Home Schooling Activities

For Teaching Social-Emotional Learning and Reading Literacy

Susanna Palomares • Patricia Rowland

Story Contributors: Tom Pettipiece, Dianne Schilling

Cover: Dave Cowan

Copyright © 2023 by Innerchoice Publishing • All rights reserved

ISBN - 10: 1-56499-104-0

ISBN - 13: 978-1-56499-104-1

INNERCHOICE Publishing
15079 Oak Chase Court
Wellington, FL 33414

www.InnerchoicePublishing.com

Activity sheets may be reproduced in quantities sufficient for distribution to children in programs utilizing *Home Schooling Activities*. All other reproduction, in any manner or for any purpose whatsoever, is explicitly prohibited without written permission. Request for such permission should be directed to INNERCHOICE PUBLISHING.

Dedication & Ackowledgment

We dedicate this book to all those parents who have shouldered the responsibility for educationg their child or children.

With grateful thanks to our friend and colleague, Michelle Brill for her expert guidance and unending encouragement.

Contents

Introduction 1

Design of the Book 3

The Importance of Social and Emotional Learning 7

How Sharing Circles Teach Life Skills 9

How to Conduct Sharing Circles 12

Tips to Help Develop Reading Literacy 16

Tips to Help Develop Social-Emotional Skills 17

Tips to Optimize Learning and Engagement 19

STORIES, ACTIVITIES & SHARING CIRCLES

RESPECT 23

KINDNESS 37

TOLERANCE 53

SERVICE TO OTHERS 71

RESPONSIBILITY 85

SELF-CONTROL 105

MAKING GOOD DECISIONS 125

Introduction

Reading, writing, speaking, and listening are all interwoven processes, and each helps build and strengthen the other. Through its variety of activities, *Home Schooling Activities For Teaching Social-Emotional Learning and Reading Literacy* fosters the relationship between these four necessary skills while helping to fully develop each. *Home Schooling Activities* provides multiple opportunities for children to read and listen to stories, to listen and respond to verbal directions, and to read and write on their personal Reflection Sheets. An important component of each unit is the Sharing Circle which provides the opportunity for children to share their ideas verbally, which is the prime method for developing oral language skills. Listening attentively to others share their thoughts in a Sharing Circle helps develop effective listening skills. Through all this sharing and listening children are learning the conventions of conversation and appropriate listening and speaking behavior. Through the Sharing Circles children also learn to clearly express their thoughts and feelings so others can understand.

Home Schooling Activities also directly affects the social and emotional development of children in a number of ways. Each unit has a social-emotional learning (SEL) theme that is fully developed and explored through the stories, activities, and Sharing Circles. As children are actively engaged in talking, sharing, listening and cooperatively doing, they are learning important skills for getting along with others. Discussions and self-reflection encourage self-awareness and self-knowledge. By following rules of good communication in the Sharing Circle and other activities, children get to express their thoughts, feelings and ideas and to learn to be respectful of, and appreciate, the ideas and feelings of others.

As a home-schooling parent, you have a dual role in developing your child's academic literacy, and social-emotional skills. As a parent, it's through the home environment you create, the behaviors you model and encourage, and the values you promote. As a teacher, you provide direct instruction through activities, experiences, and discussion.

Through its integration of language development and social-emotional learning, *Home Schooling Activities* is designed to help children grow into capable and caring young people.

Design of the Book

The Stories

The first component of each unit is a short story that embodies a specific SEL skill. There are several ways to use these stories with your child or children. Depending on their reading levels, number of children in your group, and your preferences, these stories may be read aloud to children or used for individual reading or small group read-arounds.

Several discussion questions follow each story. Use these to facilitate an exchange of reactions to the story, examination of the dilemmas and choices faced by characters in the story, and the meaning of the story in general. Always review the questions in advance and adjust them to suit the readiness of your child or children to deal with various concepts. You may want to formulate your own questions that are based on responses, learnings you would like to focus on or that are more appropriate to the level of understanding of your child or children

The Vocabulary Words

Possible new vocabulary words are listed before the first page of each story and are presented in the order in which they appear. A good way to introduce these words is to write them out for your child or children so they can see the word and then to briefly discuss each one. Ask if they are familiar with the word, and if they know what it means. Share the definitions with them and ask them to listen for each word in the story. Besides te aching the meanings of the words, you can have them alphabetize the words, circle the words as they appear in the story, use the words in sentences of their own, and/or discover synonyms or antonyms for some of the words.

The Reflection Sheets

Following each story is a "Reflection Sheet," which you may wish to duplicate and distribute to your child or children, giving them an opportunity to respond personally to the story and to write about similar situations that they have faced in their own lives. Allow them to share their answers to the questions with others and with you. This is an excellent way to help children further internalize the concepts presented in the story and unit as a whole while giving them an opportunity to write about their personal feelings and reactions to the story.

The Activities

Each unit also includes two engaging activities. These activities provide a wide range of experiences and are designed to help children internalize the values inherent in the theme of each unit.

At the conclusion of every activity, you'll find another list of "Questions for Discussion and Reflection." These questions are provided to help you involve your child or children in thinking about and summarizing the learnings derived from that particular activity. They promote thoughtful reasoning, the use of higher-level thinking skills, and internalization of knowledge and skills. Use any or all of the discussion questions provided, and feel free to ask your own questions. When planning, always allow plenty of time for discussion during and at the end of the activity.

Feel free to adapt the activities to suit the ages, ability levels, cultural/ethnic backgrounds, and interests of your child or children.

If you are home schooling only one child, the activities are still appropriate. When the activity requires interaction or sharing, you can serve as the activity "partner" with your child. You might find that it will work perfectly for your child to interact with another household member, as well, no matter their age.

The Sharing Circles

The Sharing Circle is an extremely powerful process for the development of empathy, effective listening, self-control, and many other social and emotional learning skills. Part of its value for this purpose lies in the fact that it is guided by a clear procedure, rules, and a specific topic. In addition, the process requires that children demonstrate respect, responsibility, trust, caring, and fairness as a condition of participating in every circle.

Oral language development is also an area of focus in the Sharing Circle. As the key mode of expression in each Sharing Circle, oral language is engaged in with enthusiasm because children are encouraged to express themselves and talk about their own experiences and feelings while others listen respectfully without interruption. In this way the development of oral language is strengthened and refined through its use. Furthermore, we believe oral language is a key which unlocks the door to literacy. One of the most exciting aspects of oral language is its power to stimulate other forms of expression. Children readily engage in reading, writing, acting, playing games and singing when they can read, draw, dramatize, play, and sing about things they choose to talk about first, and vice versa. In this way the Sharing Circle supports the integration of the language arts.

The "What Did You Learn About..." Page

At the conclusion of each unit, you'll find an exercise entitled "What Did You Learn About...?" These exercises comprise a very important repeating element of *Home Schooling Activities*. Reflection is an important part of learning, and these reflection pages encourage children to look back on, think about, and learn from what they have experienced in each unit. Learning brains need this time for reflection, consolidation and integration. Reflection helps develop critical thinking skills and integrates both emotional and intellectual growth. To illicit the deepest meaning allow your child or children to be creative and find their own way to express their thoughts and learning. Writing, drawing, scribbles, poetry, simple notes, etc. are all valuable.

When your child or children have completed their reflection, be sure that they have an opportunity to share their pages and tell others what they have learned. Through the process of making their thinking visible on the page and then articulating to others what they learned, they are strengthening learning pathways in the brain and committing this learning to long-term memory

The Importance of Social and Emotional Learning

Social and emotional learning (SEL) is a broad set of life skills and competencies that, when acquired, lead to the development of emotional intelligence. Just as we want children to demonstrate intelligence in academic areas, we also want them to be intelligent when they relate to others and in understanding themselves.

Children who have high levels of emotional intelligence— who manage their own feelings well, and who recognize and respond effectively to the feelings of others — are at an advantage in every area of life, whether family and peer relationships, school, sports, or community and organizational pursuits. Children with well-developed social and emotional skills are also more likely to lead happy and productive lives, and to master the habits of mind that will assure them personal and career success as adults.

Being able to effectively manage an interpersonal conflict is one example of a social skill or intelligence. Being able to demonstrate self-control when provoked and angry is an example of an emotional skill or intelligence. When children are able to use these types of social and emotional skills in their daily lives, they are demonstrating emotional intelligence. With the accumulating abundance of research and direct observation, social and emotional competencies are more and more being recognized as crucial to success in all aspects of 21st century life. School work, adult work, relationships, and general wellbeing are all dependent on having skills in such areas as self-control, goal-setting, active listening, respect for others, tolerance, and conflict and anger management. Children (and adults) lacking skills such as these struggle to perform academically and to get along with others. Conversely, children with well developed social and emotional skills perform better academically, get along better with others, and more effectively manage the inevitable challenges and setbacks of life.

This book provides you with dozens of easy-to-use and engaging activities, stories, and Sharing Circles designed to build understanding and skills in each of the following key areas of social and emotional learning:

Kindness

Tolerance

Self-Control

Respect for Self and Others

Making Good Decisions

Responsibility

Service to others

By purposefully integrating social and emotional learning into your home schooling activities, you are helping your child or children develop the skills necessary to be more effective in all areas of their lives both today and in the future.

How Sharing Circles Teach Life Skills

A safe, supportive and caring home schooling experience is something that parents and children want, value and appreciate. Because Sharing Circles provide a simple, easy-to-do process for developing positive relationships, self-awareness, and social skills, they are a prime means for fostering respect and rapport and creating an emotionally safe place while enhancing the development of critical life skills.

The Sharing Circle is a small-group discussion process in which children and adults share their feelings, experiences, and insights in response to specific, assigned topics. In a Sharing Circle everyone is expected to follow the rules that promote good communication while assuring cooperation, and trust.

The personal traits and social skills needed to grow into an effective, self-actualized person develop largely within a social environment. The nature of the Sharing Circle environment — the messages it sends to children and the behaviors it encourages and discourages are highly conducive to their development. During each Sharing Circle, all participants follow clear rules of conduct, agree to follow those rules, are supportive of one another, and experience a sense of satisfaction by complying with the rules and procedures of the circle.

The Sharing Circle is an ideal way to incorporate social and emotional learning into a home school program on a regular basis. It's structure and process provide the foundational building blocks of emotional learning.

First, the Sharing Circle process provides emotional safety, security, and unconditional acceptance to each child. Second, the topics are stimulating in their ability to provoke self-inquiry and address real-life experiences and issues and the full range of emotions associated with them. Third, the ambiance created through regular use of the Sharing Circle creates close, yet respectful, relationship leading to high levels of group cohesiveness and creativity. And finally, the immediacy of the Sharing Circle ensures that every child's contributions are heard and accepted on the spot. The attentiveness of other Circle members (children and adults) along with their verbal and non-verbal positive reactions constitute a powerful form of immediate and affirming feedback.

Skill Development

The process, rules and topics of the Sharing Circle help facilitate the social and emotional growth of children in a number of significant ways. As children follow the rules and relate to each other verbally during the Sharing Circle, they are practicing respectful listening and oral communication. By listening patiently and respectfully to others taking their turns, they are learning the important master skill of self-control. As they listen carefully while other participants ponder and discuss the various topics, children have repeated opportunities to mentally take the perspectives of others. By sharing their own experiences, thoughts, and ideas, they are gaining awareness and control over their own feelings, thoughts and behaviors, and articulating them so that others understand.

The Sharing Circle topics offered in this book address many skills, such as keeping agreements, developing responsible habits, solving problems, demonstrating respect for self and others, being loyal, being trustworthy and honest, following rules, demonstrating kindness and consideration, and resolving conflicts, etc.

Topics like these help identify core ethical values, and require children to describe incidents and behaviors from their own experience that illustrate those values. In this way Sharing Circle topics bring to awareness and reinforce important values and life skills.

The Sharing Circle allows children to confront difficult decision-making situations. In response to the topics posed, children are asked to state positions, to think about their reasons for selecting those positions, and to listen to the positions and reasoning of others.

Learning to Get Along

Through repeated experiences with the Sharing Circle, children learn to relate effectively to others, and issues related to acceptable and unacceptable behavior surface again and again. Children learn that all people have the power to influence one another. They become aware not only of how others affect them, but of the effects their behaviors have on others.

The Sharing Circle has been designed so that healthy, responsible behaviors are modeled by the adult in his or her role as circle leader. Also, the rules require that children relate responsibly and effectively to one another. The Sharing Circle brings out and affirms the positive qualities inherent in everyone and encourages children to practice effective modes of communication. Being a place where everyone is listened to, their feelings accepted, and their contributions judged as having value, the Sharing Circle teaches cooperation and promotes caring. All Sharing Circles are guided by a spirit of collaborations and trust. When children practice fair, respectful interactions with others, they benefit from the experience and are likely to employ those responsible behaviors in other life situations.

How To Conduct Sharing Circles

Sharing Circle Rules

1. **Everyone gets a turn to share, including the leader.**
2. **You can skip your turn if you wish.**
3. **Listen to the person who is sharing.**
4. **There are no interruptions, put-downs, or gossip.**
5. **Share the time equally so everyone gets a turn to speak.**

Steps for Leading a Sharing Circle

1. **State the Topic,** and then **set the stage by elaborating on the topic.** Make the topic relevant to your children. Tap into their life experiences and prior learning (Suggested elaborations are provided with each Sharing Circle Topic. Feel free to develop your own elaboration based on your knowledge of your children and what will stimulate their thinking).

2. **Facilitate the Sharing.** Make sure everyone who wants to share gets a turn to speak and is listened to respectfully and without interruption. Remind the children that there are no put-downs or gossip. What is said in the circle stays in the circle. Also, be sure to take your turn.

3. **Ask questions for reflection and learning.** At the conclusion of the Sharing phase, ask open-ended questions to stimulate thought and free discussion regarding the concepts, lessons, and other connections that can be made as a result of the sharing (Each Sharing Circle topic includes two or more discussion questions. Also ask your own questions).

Here is a more detailed look at the process of leading a Sharing Circle.

Setting the tone

The Sharing Circle provides a threat-free atmosphere where children can explore their own feelings, thoughts and behaviors and consider those of the other members of their group. When you exhibit a positive, enthusiastic attitude blended with seriousness, children will know that the Sharing Circle is an important part of the day's learning experience. By using the following communication techniques it will help to maintain rapport and provide another dimension to a caring, supportive relationship.

- Show children that you are listening and hear what they are saying
- Let them know you think highly of them and their willingness to participate
- Make a conscientious effort to promote self-esteem and confidence. The Sharing Circle is a place where everyone has the "right" answer and should always feel successful in their participation whether by speaking or simply listening.

Review the rules

The Sharing Circle rules inform children of the positive behaviors required of them and assures them of the emotional safety and equality of each participant. At the beginning of the first few sessions, and if necessary at intervals thereafter, go over the rules. From this point on demonstrate to children that you expect them to remember and abide by these rules. Convey to children that you think well of them and know they are fully capable of responsible behavior. Let them know that by participating in the Circle they are making a commitment to listen and show acceptance and respect for the other children and you. It can be helpful to display the rules for children to refer to.

State and elaborate on the topic

When you are settled in and everyone agrees to the rules, state the topic and, then in your own words, elaborate on the topic and provide examples as each Sharing Circle lesson in this book suggests. (The topic can also be written on chart paper so that children can review the topic as they need throughout the session.) You may want to expand your elaboration beyond the brief suggestions provided with more examples. This elaboration of the topic is designed to get children focused and thinking about how they will respond to the topic. By providing more than just the mere statement of the topic, the elaboration gives children a few moments to expand their thinking and to make a personal connection to the topic at hand. Add clarifying statements of your own that will help children understand the topic. Answer questions about the topic, and emphasize that there are no "right" or "wrong" responses. Finally, open the session to responses (theirs and yours). Sometimes taking your turn first helps children understand the aim of the topic. The Sharing Circle elaborations, as written in this book, are provided to give you some general ideas for opening the Sharing Circle. It's important that you adjust, expand and modify the elaboration to suit the ages, abilities, cultural/ethnic backgrounds and interests of your child or children.

Facilitate the sharing

Next, everyone takes a turn sharing their response to the topic. Remember, no one is forced to share because it's okay to pass. Everyone gets to talk about themselves, their personal experiences, thoughts, feelings, hopes and dreams as they relate to the topic. The most time in each session is devoted to this sharing phase because of its central importance.

During this time, you'll assume a dual role—that of leader and participant. As the leader, you'll make sure that everyone who wishes to speak is given the opportunity while simultaneously enforcing the rules as necessary. You'll also take your turn to speak if you wish.

Ask questions for discussion and reflection

After everyone who wants to share has done so, you'll introduce the next phase of the Sharing Circle by asking thought-provoking questions to stimulate free discussion and higher-level thinking. As John Dewey, the early 20th century educational leader and reformer said "We do not learn from experience, we learn from reflecting on experience". Each Sharing

Circle lesson concludes with several culminating discussion questions designed to foster reflection and self-awareness. It's in this phase that children are able to crystallize learning and to understand the relevance of the discussion to their daily lives. You may want to formulate your own questions that are based on the responses you heard, relevant learning's you would like to focus on, or that are more appropriate to the level of understanding in your child or children. Use your judgment to determine exactly what questions to ask.

Close the circle

The ideal time to end a session is when the discussion question phase reaches natural closure. You may want to thank children for positive behaviors that were demonstrated during the session. Don't thank specific children for speaking, as doing so might convey the impression that speaking is more appreciated than listening. Both are important.

Note: If you are conducting a Sharing Circle with only one child, you can still talk about the topic and follow the same rules of good listening. You and your child each take a turn listening attentively to each other and then discussing together what you have learned or noticed from the sharing. If you have another person at home who will be available, the Sharing Circle can be conducted as a threesome or family group. This helps to strengthen family bonds while teaching and supporting important social, emotional, and character skills.

Tips to Help Develop Reading Literacy

Have books available

Provide books that children can comfortably read. When children read accurately and understand what they are reading, their chances of reading success increase significantly, and obviously makes reading much more enjoyable. Besides educating, books should also entertain. Make sure books are available that children want to read just for the pure pleasure of doing so. Provide books that cover a wide range of topics. Encourage children to read and re-read favorite books. These repeated readings improve children's fluency and comprehension. Allow children to read and discuss what they are reading with others, either children or adults.

Read to children often

Read to children often – everyday, if you can. You'll model fluent reading as you read and re-read books to them. Even though they may be able to read on their own, it's important to find time to read books and stories that children enjoy. This helps them learn vocabulary and pronunciation while they listen to examples of fluent reading.

Make reading active

Use readers' theatre to promote reading. Have children "act out" stories that they read or hear. Creating scripts, designing costumes, and staging make a story interactive and can really bring all dimensions of reading literacy alive.

Tips to Help Develop Social-Emotional Skills

Model the Behavior You Want

Children learn a lot about relationships and how to positively interact with others by observing the behavior of the adults around them. Make sure children see you demonstrating healthy social-emotional skills such as sharing with others, patiently waiting your turn, saying please and thank you, and calmly responding to intense situations. Remember that the first step in developing healthy social-emotional skills in your children is for you to model emotionally intelligent behavior.

Talk About Feelings and Emotions

Help children identify and label what they are feeling (angry, sad, happy, excited, etc.) When a child is experiencing an intense emotion, try to avoid saying things like, *don't be mad* (*or sad*), or *calm down*. When children hear these things, they are being taught that some emotions are bad and shouldn't be expressed or shared in any way. Help children to recognize and name their feelings. It then becomes easier to help them find appropriate ways in which to express and manage their feelings and behaviors effectively.

Be A Good Listener

Take time for age-appropriate, meaningful conversations and really listen to what children have to say. Encourage them to share their ideas and opinions. Simply by listening, rather than giving advice, you can help them solve problems and process intense experiences. When you are actively listening, you encourage expression, and reflect back what you think your child is feeling (ex., *You seem angry that Matt took your baseball without asking.*) Since listening is a core competency in the social-emotional realm, it's important to remember that when you model and demonstrate good listening, your child is also learning how to be a good listener.

Nurture Self Esteem

Give plenty of opportunities for children to make choices and have responsibilities. Provide positive support and encouragement while fostering age appropriate independence. Acknowledge accomplishment and appreciation of a job well done. Keep the focus on what is being done right rather than what is wrong. Praising children for their effort rather than the outcome teaches them that effort matters and that regardless of the outcome, you are proud of them. This helps build their self confidence, persistence, and resiliency in the face of challenges and failure.

Tips to Optimize Learning and Engagement

Create A Supportive and Encouraging Environment

Positive relationships are key in any endeavor, especially so when children are in an educational learning environment. Children thrive when they get personal acknowledgment and attention each day, and they feel safe in expressing their thoughts and feelings An emotionally safe and supportive environment encourages children to try new things, make mistakes and communicate thoughts and feelings without fear of judgment or punishment. Make learning a positive experience and create a low stress supportive environment where children are encouraged, listened to, and in which they feel valued.

Activate Prior Knowledge

The latest research into how the human brain learns is showing that it is essential to use children's life experiences, prior knowledge, and memories as a foundation upon which new learnings are built. In order for a new learning to be retained it has to connect to something the child already has some experience with. Asking questions to get children thinking about what they already know about the topic you will be teaching is an important way to bring personal relevance and meaning to the topic. At the beginning of any activity, or story, ask questions that will help children recall and identify what they already know about the topic. For example, if you are beginning the "Service to Others" unit before you read the story ask children to think about a time they helped someone out. When beginning the "Kindness" unit, you could ask children to recall kind acts that others have done for them.

When introducing each Sharing Circle Topic to children, you will be providing an elaboration that naturally helps each child to personally relate the topic to his or her life experiences. Topic elaborations are provided for each Sharing Circle in this book, but feel free to create your own elaborations that are aligned with your awareness of your children's prior knowledge and experience.

Tap into feelings

Everything the human brain learns is filtered through emotions. Emotion is the gate-keeper to learning. Learning and emotion are so intertwined that they constantly influence each other. Learning takes place easily when it is attached to strong feelings. Learning is enhanced when the activities, Sharing Circles, and stories are presented and performed in a joyous, fun, and exciting fashion. Laughter, group interaction, and just plain fun are good for learning, lowering stress, and making your home school program a place where children want to be.

All the activities presented in *Home Schooling Activities* are designed to promote learning and involvement by being fun and engaging experiences for children, and you.

Make time for movement and exercise

The more active and physically engaged children are the better learning outcomes are. Having children take walking breaks throughout the day and even during lessons, allows them to retain information and revitalizes and increases attention span as well. Build movement and physical engagement into lessons whenever possible, and take regular breaks during direct instruction.

STORIES, ACTIVITIES & SHARING CIRCLES

RESPECT

"Respect children because they're human beings and they deserve respect, and they'll grow up to be better people."

Benjamin Spock

Tips for Teaching Respect:

When you speak with respect to children, they learn respect. When you speak with disrespect, they learn that just as well. If you want them to do it, you must do it too.

When you see or hear your child or children using respectful language and making respectful choices, recognize it and praise him or her for it, and make sure to call your child on disrespectful behavior, too.

Discuss the concept of respect with your child. Point out situations when you observe others being respected and disrespected. Ask your child how he or she would feel being the recipient of the respectful or disrespectful actions.

Remind your child to be polite by saying things such as, "Please" and "Thank you." Explain that good manners are a way to show respect to others.

Vocabulary Words

- Ignore
- Humiliated
- Avoiding
- Amazing
- Anxious
- Courteous

How the Turkey Became a Star

Todd was a turkey. But not all the time. Sometimes he was a squirrel and other times he was just a weird stupid jerk.

At least Ralph thought so, because that's what Ralph called Todd every time he saw him. Ralph was a bully.

One day Todd was walking with Nathan through the park on the way to the ball field, when Ralph, who was about a foot taller than Todd, deliberately bumped Todd, as he passed. Everybody saw that Ralph did it on purpose.

"Hey Punk," he said meanly. "Watch where you're going."

Todd tried to ignore him and kept on walking.

"Hey Stupid! Stop when I'm talking to you."

Todd stopped and looked at Nathan. He was scared. Ralph came over and hit Todd on the shoulder as hard as he could. By now, all the kids on the ball field were looking at Todd. He tried but couldn't hold back the tears. It hurt and worse then that, he felt helpless, alone and humiliated.

"You little wimp," Ralph said. "Look at the crybaby. Crybaby!"

Todd ran off afraid everyone would notice he was crying.

This sort of thing was common. Every time Ralph saw Todd he did something to Todd. He would run up behind Todd and poke him in the back. He'd grab anything Todd was carrying and throw it into the trash while everyone watched.

Occasionally, Todd would say, "Knock it off, Ralph" or "Leave me alone!" But this only seemed to make Ralph more keen to pick on Todd. The only thing that worked was to stay out of Ralph's way.

In short, Todd spent most of his time avoiding Ralph. As a result, his friendships suffered and everyone accused him of daydreaming. Ralph was running Todd's life. The only thing that made life bearable was thinking about summer.

That summer Todd spent several weeks at camp. He created computer games. He learned to spell backwards as fast as he could frontwards. He swam and hiked, and he painted colorful pictures of horses and houses. He sang, acted in skits, and spoke in front of the group. He even learned how to make himself seem heavy or light to pick up, just by picturing in his mind he was an anchor or a feather.

Todd learned that his brain could do amazing things. For the summer, Todd was happy. He felt good about himself and made lots of new friends. The camp was called "Starshine" and Todd was indeed a star!

When Todd's mother picked him up from camp she asked him how he thought it would go with Ralph this year. Todd felt anxious. He was already worried about Ralph. But Todd's mother said, "You're a star, Todd. You don't need Ralph calling you names or bothering you again. You're too bright and too confident for that!"

Todd thought about what his mother said and thought back to all the things he had learned over the summer. He realized that he was strong and capable. He knew that now he had control over how he thought and reacted to things, and that Ralph wasn't going to be able to bully him anymore.

Ralph was there the first day Todd got back to the park and looked meanly at Todd when they passed each other. But before he could say anything, Todd stopped, smiled confidently, and said, "Ralph, don't start anything, because it won't work. You don't have to like me, but it is time you started showing me some respect."

Ralph took a step backwards. He sensed immediately that Todd had changed, and it threw him completely. Ralph mumbled and growled and shuffled his feet, but he couldn't think of anything to say.

Todd stood his ground for a full minute. Finally, he said cheerfully, "See ya around, Ralph," and walked away.

Ralph didn't know a lot about respect. Most of what he did know, he had learned the hard way. It took him a long time to understand what he had learned from Todd that day. Though, just to be safe, he steered clear of Todd while he was figuring it out.

Eventually Ralph learned that being courteous and respectful toward people got him all the attention he needed, without the need to constantly prove that he was bigger or tougher than everyone else. He even learned to be friendly.

Four or five years later, when Ralph's bully streak had completely faded away, Todd and Ralph became good friends.

Questions for Discussion and Reflection:

1. How did Ralph's bullying behavior affect Todd?
2. Why didn't Ralph show respect for Todd in the beginning?
3. Do you think Ralph respected himself? Why or why not?
4. What is respectful behavior?
5. Does everyone deserve respect, or is respect something that must be earned?
6. When you lose respect for someone, does that mean that you can treat the person badly? Why or why not?

How the Turkey Became a Star

Reflection Sheet

Think about the story of Todd and Ralph. What did you learn from the story? Read and answer the following questions. Be prepared to talk about your answers with others.

1. What did Todd learn about himself at camp?

2. What did Todd do that helped to change Ralph's attitude toward him?

3. What does it mean to respect someone?

4. How do you show respect for others?

How We Show Respect
Interviews, Drawing and Discussion

This activity teaches children to:

— identify respectful actions.
— describe an incident in which they demonstrated respect.
— creatively symbolize expressions of respect.

You will need:

art paper; scratch paper and pencils; colored marker or crayons; glue; decorative materials such as stickers, sequins, buttons, etc. (optional)

Directions:

Begin by asking your child/children to think of things that people do to show respect for one another. Focus on small courtesies like greeting a person, saying please and thank you, holding a door, letting someone go first, and shaking hands. Share this with the children:

I've heard that some coaches insist that their players shake hands with the members of the opposing team after every game, regardless of whether they win or lose. Why would a coach do that? What message does the coach want to send the other team? What do the players learn by doing this?

After your child/children have had a few minutes to talk about this display of respect, announce that they are going to participate in an activity about respect, but in this activity instead of shaking hands, they'll draw hands.

Have the children work in pairs. (If you are working with one child, you can be the partner.) Distribute the paper and pencils.

Instruct your child/children to take turns tracing each other's hand on a sheet of art paper. Point out that the drawing they end up with will not be of their own hand, but of their partner's hand. When they have finished tracing, explain the next step (in your own words):

Interview your partner to find out how your partner shows respect for other people. See if your partner can remember a specific time when they said or did something that demonstrated respect for a particular person. Take notes on your scratch paper. Then let your partner interview you. When both of you have finished, use what you've learned to illustrate the tracing of your partner's hand to show the respectful things your partner does. Use letters, symbols, pictures, and other decorations. Your illustration can symbolize lots of respectful actions, or it can tell the story of one particular incident. Decide who will be the first interviewer and get started.

Make available the art materials. Write out the following interview questions for your child/children to see and refer to during their interviews:

Interview Questions:

- How do you show respect for other people?

- Can you remember a specific time when you did something for another person that showed respect? What happened?

When your child/children have finished their drawings, instruct them to introduce their partner by showing their hand drawing and describing their partner's respectful actions to others.

Lead a culminating group discussion.

Questions for Discussion and Reflection:

1. A picture of two hands shaking is often used as a symbol of mutual respect and peace. Why do you think that is?
2. What are some other ways of showing respect that we included in our drawings?
3. If you offered to shake someone's hand and that person refused, what would you think?
4. Why is it important to show respect for others?
5. What would life be like if no one showed respect for anyone else.

Respected Friends
Writing, Art, and Discussion

This activity teaches children to:
—recognize respect as a critically important ingredient in friendship.
—contemplate healthy friendships through art and writing.

What you need:
art materials of your choosing; writing materials

Directions:

Prior to beginning the activity, write the following words for your child/children to see:
- trustworthy
- loyal
- responsible
- honest
- kind
- considerate
- sensitive
- generous
- fair
- caring
- dignified

Introduce the activity by telling your child/children about a childhood friendship you had with an individual you greatly respected. Describe the individual using adjectives similar to those listed. Include an anecdote or two to illustrate the character of your friend and emphasize the degree to which this person's actions and attributes caused you to respect them. Answer any questions your child/children have while continuing to illustrate the importance of respect between friends.

In your own words, say: *Does this make you think of someone you really like and respect? Close your eyes and bring someone to mind. (Pause for a few moments.) Perhaps you can think of a time when this person made you proud that he or she was your friend. Maybe you found out how your friend helped someone who needed help, kept a promise, met a responsibility, told the truth when it needed to be told, or stuck up for you. Perhaps you remember a nerve-wracking situation that your friend handled very well, when others might have gone to pieces.*

Listen to your child/children's responses. Then explain that they are going to draw pictures illustrating these friendships. In your own words, explain: *Show something your friend did — an action that caused you to respect him or her. You can put yourself in the picture, too. Perhaps you want to illustrate something very meaningful that your friend did for you. This friend does not have to be your age; he or she can be a family member, someone older or younger than you, even an adult — anyone whom you respect and consider a friend.*

As your child/children draw, engaging them in conversation about their illustrations. Suggest they consider using cartoon-style speech bubbles to show what is being said.

Distribute writing materials and instruct your child/children to tell the same story in words. Point to the adjectives you listed and read them together, urging them to use any that describe their friend. Tell them to explain who their friend is, how the friendship started, how long it has lasted, and why they respect this person. Give some examples:

I respect Cindy a lot because she is usually kind and considerate to other people. She is always one of the first to be friendly to new kids in the neighborhood.

I respect Hahn because he is honest and fair, and can be trusted to keep his promises. He promised to help me with fractions and now I'm doing much better in math.

As your child/children write, offer any assistance and encouragement needed. Conclude the activity by inviting your child/children to read their stories and show their illustrations to others. Encourage questions and offer positive comments at the end of each presentation. Finally, collect the illustrations and stories and prepare a display under the banner: "Friends We Respect and Why"

Questions for Discussion and Reflection:

1. What are some reasons we gave for respecting our friends?
2. Do the friends we described show respect for others? What are some of their respectful behaviors?
3. Why is it important to show respect for others?
4. Is it important to you that your friends respect you? ...Why?
5. What did you learn from this activity about how to be a respected friend?

What I Like and Respect About Someone

A Sharing Circle

This Sharing Circle teaches children to:

— identify likable, respectable qualities in others.
— distinguish between feelings of liking and respect.
— describe something they can do to become more likable or worthy of respect.

Introduce the Topic:

Today our topic is, "What I Like and Respect About Someone." Each of us is going to think of a person for whom we feel admiration and respect, and try to pinpoint at least one quality in that person that causes us to have those feelings. Maybe the person works hard, or is very honest, or kind, or smart. Perhaps you like the person because he or she is friendly and accepts you the way you are, and perhaps you respect this person because he or she always keeps promises, treats people well, or gets involved in projects at church or in the community. Try to be specific. If you say that the person you like and respect is nice, try to describe one nice thing this person has done recently. Think it over for a few moments. The topic is, "What I Like and Respect About Someone."

Questions for Discussion and Reflection:

1. What kinds of things did we name that caused us to respect another person? ...to like another person?
2. What is the difference between liking a person and respecting the same person?
3. Can you like a person you don't respect? ...respect a person you don't like? Explain.
4. Which is more important to you, being liked or being respected? Why?
5. What have you learned from this session that will help you become a more likable person? ...a person others will respect?

How I Show Respect Toward Others

A Sharing Circle

This Sharing Circle teaches children to:

— identify specific behaviors that show respect.
— explain the difference between feeling respect and demonstrating it.
— state that how they act toward another person is a choice they make.

Introduce the Topic:

Our topic today is about showing respect, which is not the same as having respect. When you have respect for someone, you feel it inside; when you show respect, your actions demonstrate it. Our topic is, "How I Show Respect Toward Others."

Maybe you show your respect for people by being courteous and polite. Another way to show respect is to listen attentively when a person talks and not ridicule or make fun of what he says. Facial expressions can show respect or the lack of it; so can posture, gestures, and other types of body language. At times, showing respect can also mean leaving a person alone, not bothering her, allowing her to believe in, talk about, and do what she thinks is right for her. You might want to picture in your mind someone whom you respect and then think about how you act toward that person that shows your respect. Our topic is, "How I Show Respect Toward Others."

Questions for Discussion and Reflection:

1. What respectful actions were mentioned most during our circle?
2. How do you feel when someone shows respect for you?
3. Why is it important to demonstrate our respect for others?
4. What is the difference between having respect and showing it?
5. Who decides how you will act toward another person?

What Did You Learn About Respect?

Use this page to think about and record the things you have learned about respect. You can write, draw pictures, scribble and doodle, create a poem, or anything else that has meaning to you and will help you remember what you have learned.

When you finish, show this page to someone else and explain what you have learned.

KINDNESS

"You can't assume that kindness is an inherited trait. It's learned behavior."

Katie Couric

Tips for Teaching Kindness:

If your child sees someone being treated unkindly (or your child is being unkind to someone), ask what it would be like to be in the other person's shoes. Ask how it would feel if someone treated him or her that way?

If you give or receive a special acknowledgment or "thank you", share your feelings and gratitude with your child. The importance of kindness will sink in when your child sees how important kind words are to you.

Model thoughtful and kind behaviors. Everything you say and do teaches your child something. Be mindful of what you are teaching. Be kind, thoughtful, and polite. Sincerely compliment others. Etc.

Talk with your child about people you think are kind to others. Together, describe those behaviors, and discuss ways he or she can act in those kind ways too.

Vocabulary Words

- Baffled
- Touted
- Serenade
- Retorted
- Anticipation
- Scanned
- Fuming
- Snide
- Cast
- Boasted
- Debut
- Elated
- Vibrancy
- Forlorn

Stardom

"The summer community theater will be starting soon," said Heather to her friend, Sally. "I am so excited, aren't you Sally?"

"Oh yes, it was so much fun being in a play and performing just like a real actor!" replied Sally.

"I think I am going to be a famous actor when I grow up. I'll be as famous as Marilyn Monroe," bragged Heather.

"Who?" asked Sally with a confused look on her face.

"Never mind," snapped Heather. "Let's go to the Community Center and check out the audition dates and what the play is going to be this year." The two girls started off down the street toward the Community Center.

When they reached the Community Center, there was a large group of boys and girls of all ages standing around chattering. Sally and Heather met up with some friends their own age. Apparently the sign up for auditions was about to begin. Heather and Sally were baffled. They were sure the summer theatre started in July and here it was the beginning of June. "Why so early this year?" thought Heather out loud. She soon got her answer when Sally's older brother, Billy, appeared through the crowd and informed them that this year's production will be a musical with a real live orchestra.

"This is no sissy play, ladies," touted Billy. "We are going to have an orchestra with horns, violins, bases, and ALL the instruments! It's going to be a really great production this year and a longer rehearsal time is needed. That's why the sign up for auditions starts today!" he continued.

Both Heather and Sally were thanking their lucky stars that they had shown up. Ms. Mary Catherine, the theater's director, appeared before the group and began sharing details about the musical and the audition process. "I am very excited about this year's production. Our play is a musical and will include singing and dancing. The title is *Eagle's Serenade*. It is about a young American Indian boy who becomes his tribe's hero when he finds an the Indian maiden who is lost in the forest." explained Ms. Mary Catherine. "Here is the sign up sheet for auditions. Auditions will be held for 2 days. Next to your name identify whether you are signing up to audition for a dancer, singer, or main role. We will post the times and days for auditioning by the end of the week." she finished explaining.

A line started forming to sign up for the auditions. As Heather and Sally waited in line, they overheard a boy behind them say, "W-w-wow, wow, th-th-this is e-e-exciting! Hi my n-n-name is R-r-robby." said the new boy in the neighborhood.

Heather and Sally turned around and stared at Robby for a few seconds. They quickly turned away while Heather bragged to Sally, "I am going to audition for the Indian maiden. I will be perfect for the part!"

Sally retorted, "We will see. You know you will have to sing too, and singing is not something you're good at." Heather just rolled her eyes at Sally and looked back at Robby.

Robby smiled at Heather. Trying to start a conversation with Heather, Robby stuttered, "Y-y-you are going to t-t-tr-try out for the m-m-maiden? I w-w-want to be-e-e the Indian hero."

Heather turned back to face Sally and started laughing while making fun of him. "He has some nerve trying out for the main role. He can't even speak rrrrr-right!" Ms. Mary Catherine, the director, heard Heather's teasing and shot her a nasty look. Heather bowed her head, looked down to the ground and continued to laugh quietly. Meanwhile Robby just stood behind the girls waiting for his turn to sign up.

When the auditions were completed, Ms. Mary Catherine informed the group of eager actors, that it would take another few days before roles would be assigned. There would then be an assigned role listing on the door of the Community Center by the end of the week. Everyone was filled with anticipation and high hopes.

It seemed like a long week of waiting for the list of role assignments to be posted, but the day finally came. Heather and Sally went with excitement to the Community Center and found a large crowd gathered in front of the posting. Heather made her way to the front and quickly scanned for her name. Much to her disappointment, she was assigned as the understudy for the Indian maiden. As Heather made her way back to where Sally was, she was fuming mad. "I only got the understudy part for the Indian maiden. And guess who got the role of the Indian hero? Robby, that stupid kid who can't even talk rrr-right! This play is going to be a flop," she said in a loud and angry voice.

Sally was embarrassed to be around Heather as she was ranting and raving. She was even more embarrassed when she saw that Robby and Ms. Mary Catherine were standing right behind Heather as she carried on. Sally tried to warn Heather, but Heather kept carrying on with her angry disappointment and snide remarks.

Ms. Mary Catherine came up behind Heather and put her hand on Heather's shoulder. "I understand that you may be disappointed in your role assignment of understudy Heather, but that is an important role" she explained. She then continued, "I am disappointed to hear your put downs regarding Robby and his role in the play. It is very unkind of you to make fun of him and you will be very surprised by his talent as we begin rehearsals."

Heather mumbled an apology to Ms. Mary Catherine. "I expect you to be at every rehearsal and have a change in attitude as well," she lectured.

"Yes, Ma'am," Heather replied.

Rehearsals began the following week. Every day from 2 to 4, and for two and a half long months, the boys and girls enthusiastically rehearsed their parts. Sally was cast as a dancing Indian girl which she was very pleased about. Heather reluctantly was at every rehearsal learning her lines and waiting for her turn to perform.

"I think this play is going to be spectacular!" Sally exclaimed after every rehearsal.

"Yeah, yeah," Heather replied in a sour tone. "I am sure it is going to be a waste of time for me. I won't even get to be on stage because I am the understudy," complained Heather.

"Come on, Heather. Think positive. You may get your turn," Sally replied encouragingly. "And aren't you surprised by Robby's performance. He sings so beautifully and doesn't seem to stutter when he sings or with his lines," Sally boasted.

"Yeah, yeah, he seems to be able to talk rrr-right now!" Heather snarked.

Two and a half months of rehearsals finally came to an end and the production was about to make its debut. The day before opening night Heather got a phone call from Ms. Mary Catherine explaining that she would be performing on opening night because the other actor had come down with the flu. Heather was elated but nervous because she had lost interest in the play and did not practice her lines very much at home.

Opening night was so well attended by the community, that it was a packed house. As the curtain rose and the lights shined on the stage, the audience clapped with delight. The play began with an exciting Indian tribal dance. The costumes, music and dancers lit up the stage with vibrancy. Heather stood up stage of the tribal dance looking nervously out to the audience. When the dance was completed Robby entered the stage and walked over to the Indian maiden, Heather. "Why are you so forlorn?" said the young Indian. Silence... Heather could not say her lines! More moments of silence passed with Heather standing frozen on stage. Robby realized her moment of fear and just broke into the song that was to be sung after the Indian maiden's response. Robby's singing was so beautiful that nobody noticed Heather could not say her lines. The audience applauded loudly after the song, and Heather was able to pick up her lines after the applause died down. The play continued perfectly until the end.

Everyone loved the musical and there were three curtain calls before the crowd quieted down. Between the second and the third curtain calls, Heather broke down in tears. With Robby by her side, she gripped his hand to rise and take another bow. The curtain closed for the last time. Heather hugged Robby and said though her tears, "Thank you Robby, you saved me. You sang so beautifully and you were able to say all your lines. You were fantastic!"

"Th-th-thanks, He-he-heather. I-i-i guess I am de-de-destined t-t-to be an actor, j-j-just like Ji-Jimmy St-Stewart and J-j-James Earl J-j-Jones." responded Robby with a big smile on his face.

"Yes, you are!" Heather cried while giving him a big hug. "I am so sorry I said such unkind things about you. You are unbelievably fabulous. I want to be your friend!"

"Okay," replied Robby giving her a big hug back.

Questions for Discussion and Reflection:

1. Why was Heather unkind to Robby?
2. How do you think Robby felt when Heather laughed and mocked him?
3. Was Sally unkind to Robby?
4. How did Heather feel about her part in the play?
5. How do you think Heather felt during opening night?
6. How did Heather feel during the curtain calls?
7. What does it mean to be kind?
8. What is the "Golden Rule?"
9. How can we use the Golden Rule to guide our actions toward other people?
10. What are some specific ways we can show each other kindness?

Stardom

Reflection Sheet

Think about the story, "Stardom." What thoughts do you have about the characters? How did you react to the things they said and did? Use this page to write down your thoughts as you answer the questions.

2. **Think of someone you know who is very kind. What are some of the kind things this person does?**

1. **Have you ever been the object of teasing or put-downs? How did you feel and what did you do?**

3. **Describe an act of kindness that you have done for someone recently:**

4. **Think of three kind acts that you can do for friends or family members during the next week. List them here:**

A Book of Kindness
Writing and Art Activity

This activity teaches children to:

— define the term kindness.
— brainstorm examples of kind deeds.
— describe a kind act they did or received.

You will need:

writing materials; drawing paper; colored marking pens, crayons, or pencils; glue; a large three-ring binder

Directions:

Write the word kindness and show it to your child/children. Ask them to help you define its meaning. In the process, make these points about kindness:

- Kindness is a quality that is developed from being kind.
- Being kind means being considerate, thoughtful, or helpful.
- An act of kindness is something you do. It is a deed or behavior. It's possible to have kind thoughts and feelings, but they are private until you express them in an act of kindness.
- A kind act is always done voluntarily, not because it is required.

Ask your child/children to think of examples of kind acts. Write out their suggestions so they can see and refer back to them. Encourage a variety of ideas, by asking questions like "What are some kind acts you can do for a friend? ...brother or sister? ...parent? ...neighbor? ...grandparent? ...a stranger? ...the environment?

Help your child/children to identify kind acts like these:

— make friends with a new child
— offer to share things
— talk to or play with kids who seem left out

— give someone a compliment
— read a story to a younger child
— visit senior citizens in the neighborhood
— help a friend do his or her chores
— help a friend solve a tough math problem
— surprise your parent by doing an "extra" chore
— hold a door for someone
— pick up trash when you see it lying around

Announce that they are now going to write about and draw an act of kindness they've done — or one that someone else has done for them, and then assemble it all into a "Book of Kindness". Distribute writing and drawing materials. In your own words, explain:

Describe the kind act, tell who did it, and for whom it was done. You don't have to mention names, just use words like "friend," "teacher," "sister," or "older person." Then write about the feelings of the person who did the kind deed, and the feelings of the person who received it. On another sheet of paper draw a picture that shows the kind act being done.

Help your child/children correct the spelling and grammar in their stories in order for them to complete a rewrite. When finished, have them share their stories and pictures. As a final step, have them assemble their stories and drawings, and then place all of the finished work in the three-ring binder. Have them create a cover page titled, "Book of Kindness," and make it available so that it can be looked at and referred to often.

Questions for Discussion and Reflection:

1. Why is it important to try to turn kind thoughts into kind deeds?
2. When you have a kind thought about someone, how can you express it?
3. Can chores and assignments ever be acts of kindness? Why or why not?
4. Why do acts of kindness have to be voluntary?

Kindness Coupons
A Writing and Design Project

This activity teaches children to:
— identify kind acts that can be done for different people.
— commit to future acts of kindness by describing them in writing.

You will need:
samples of coupons or coupon books (optional); 8 1/2-inch by 11-inch sheets of sturdy white paper cut horizontally into three equal pieces (8 1/2 by 3 2/3); several sheets of colored construction paper cut to the same size or slightly larger; colored markers, pencils or crayons; decorative stickers (optional); stapler; chart paper

Directions:
Write the headings **Parents, Friend, Brother/Sister, Grandparents, Neighbors** on the chart paper. Ask your child/children to help you list acts of kindness that they could do for each of these people. For example:

Parents
wash dishes
give a massage
give a big hug
watch the baby
give a compliment
carry the groceries
clean and sort a drawer or shelf

When you have generated several items under each heading, announce that they are going to make a Kindness Coupon Book to give to some other person. Explain that each page will have a coupon that can be torn out and redeemed for a specific act of kindness. A description of the kind action will be written on the page, and they can decorate the coupons with borders, fancy lettering, symbols, drawings, or stickers (if available).

Give each child six to ten sheets of cut white paper and two pieces of cut colored construction paper. Have them make a sharp crease in each white sheet about 1–1/2 inches from the left edge. Tell them not to draw or write on the left section because this is where the coupons will be stapled together. The crease will allow for easy tearing.

Make two coupons yourself to demonstrate the process. On each coupon write or print a description of a kind action and any instructions for receiving it. For example, "5-Minute Back Massage — Good any evening 6:00 - 8:00 p.m." Decorate with a drawing of a hand or some other symbol. Make a second sample. Then place the coupons between two pieces of colored construction paper to create front and back covers. Staple the left edge securely. On the front cover, print "Kindness Coupon Book" in large dark letters.

Have your child/children decide who the recipient of their "Kindness Coupon Book" will be (e.g. a friend, cousin, grandparent, neighbor). Make the art materials available, and encourage collaboration.

Discuss how and when they will present their coupon book to their chosen recipient.

Follow up with your child/children to have them share what happened when they presented their coupon books.

Questions for Discussion and Reflection:

1. Why do acts of kindness — even very small ones — make the recipient happy?
2. Do you sometimes need permission before doing something for a person? When?
3. What could you say or do if the recipient of your kindness coupon book turned in a coupon when you didn't feel like doing the kind act?
4. How does it make you feel when you perform a kind act?

Variation:

You may prefer to have your child/children make a coupon book to carry with them, rather than give to someone else. The coupons are torn out by the child and given to different people one at a time, then redeemed by those people for specific acts of kindness. This method allows the child to control the process, which ensures that the kind acts are always voluntary. Be sure to provide the opportunity for your child/children to share when they have given out a coupon and to tell what happened.

A Time I Felt Sorry for Someone Who Was Put Down

A Sharing Circle

This Sharing Circle teaches children to:

— express empathy for the feelings of another person.
— describe some of the negative effects of put-downs.
— explain why people use put-downs.
— describe ways of avoiding the habit of putting others down.

Introduce the topic:

Today, we're going to talk about put-downs and how they affect people. Our topic is, "A Time I Felt Sorry for Someone Who Was Put Down." Unfortunately, people seem to put each other down a lot these days. In addition, we see put-downs all the time on television. Many of those put-downs are supposed to come across as clever and funny. This is unfortunate, because put-downs hurt people — even those that are intended as jokes.

Try to remember a time when you observed someone say or do something that made another person feel bad. Maybe the put-down was done as a joke or perhaps it was intended to be hurtful. The incident may have occurred anywhere, in the neighborhood, at the supermarket or shopping mall, or somewhere else. Without mentioning any names, tell us what happened, how you reacted, and how you think the person who was put down felt. Think it over for a few moments. The topic is, "A Time I Felt Sorry for Someone Who Was Put Down."

Questions for Discussion and Reflection:

1. How did most of us react to seeing another person put down?
2. How do you feel when someone puts you down?
3. Why do people put each other down?
4. How can you prevent yourself from getting in the "put-down" habit?

Something I Did to Make Someone Feel Good

A Sharing Circle

This Sharing Circle teaches children to:

— identify specific words and actions that create good feelings in others.
— accept credit for good and kind deeds.
— explain how acts of kindness benefit themselves and others.

Introduce the Topic:

Today's topic is a very broad one that can be discussed in many ways. It is, "Something I Did to Make Someone Feel Good." You see what I mean? You have probably done hundreds of things to make other people feel good. Just tell us about one.

Maybe you gave someone a flower, a present, or a compliment. Perhaps you hugged a friend who was feeling bad, or offered to relieve a parent of a chore or errand. Sometimes telling a joke can make someone feel good. So can telling a person what a good job he or she did, or saying, "I like you" or "I love you." Describe what you said or did and how you felt inside. The topic is, "Something I Did to Make Someone Feel Good."

Questions for Discussion and Reflection:

1. How do you feel when you know you've made someone feel good?
2. Usually, when a person feels good, everyone who comes in contact with that person benefits. Can you explain how that happens?
3. If everyone in our group tried to make one extra person feel good each day, how would our group benefit?

What Did You Learn About Kindness?

Use this page to think about and record the things you have learned about kindness. You can write, draw pictures, scribble and doodle, create a poem, or anything else that has meaning to you and will help you remember what you have learned.

When you finish, show this page to someone else and explain what you have learned.

TOLERANCE

"Just imagine how boring life would be if we were all the same. My idea of a perfect world is one in which we really appreciate each others differences."

Barbra Striesand

Tips for Teaching Tolerance:

Talk about differences respectfully. Talk about the differences among your family and friends (hair color, skin color, personal likes and dislikes), and use the opportunity to talk about how it's good that people are different. You could also discuss how people are the same as well (i.e. you have blonde hair and your friend has brown hair, but you are both girls and you both have two eyes, two ears, one mouth, etc.).

Promote openness and respect by demonstrating empathy and compassion through your words and actions. Besides not letting your child bully or tease someone else, watch what you say yourself! Treat others with respect, and your child will, too. Even comments about your own body can lead a child to make judgments about other people.

Encourage self-confidence. A child who is confident about him or herself will be more likely to embrace differences and see the value in others.

Vocabulary Words

- Imbedded
- Research
- Snorted
- Gesturing
- Imitating

Randy Learns About Tolerance

Tolerance. The word was everywhere. In big plastic letters on the sign outside the main office, just below where it said Kennedy Elementary School. Lettered across the top of bulletin boards in all the classrooms. Imbedded in colorful posters hung throughout the halls. On the inside curved walls of the school buses. Tolerance — the word of the month.

Well, it was more than a word. Tolerance was the moral value of the month. Last month the moral value was Kindness and the month before it was Respect. In January, the first month to have a value, all the signs said Honesty.

On Monday, Ms. Bartels told her 5th-grade class to look up the meaning of the word. "After you've done your research, be thinking about what tolerance means to you," she said. "Next week, I'll ask you to share some of your ideas."

"It's hard not to think about it," eleven-year-old Randy sighed to himself. "Tolerance is everywhere you look.

"Have you seen the new boy who moved in on the corner?" Randy asked his mother. "He looks funny."

"Yes, I've seen him from a distance," answered Corrine. "He has come from Africa to live with the Stewarts. He may look a little different from most of the folks we know. Maybe he even does some things a little differently. But inside I'm sure he's a lot like you."

"He'll probably go to my school. He's in for trouble if he does," Randy thought out loud.

"What do you mean?" demanded Corrine. "Why would there be trouble?"

"Because he's different, Mom. If you don't fit in, you get teased. Kids say things."

Randy's mother snorted angrily and slammed her open palm on the kitchen counter. "Something is seriously wrong if we can't have a little tolerance for each other's differences," she said. "I expect you to be nice to that new boy, Randy. And by tolerance I mean accepting other people just as they are" said Corrine sternly. "Everybody can't be just like us."

Sure enough, the new boy from the Stewart house was at school the very next day. And he was in Randy's class.

"Children, this is Josephat Nmbura. Josephat is from Tanzania, which is a country in Africa," said Ms. Bartels, gesturing toward the thin, dark boy seated near the front of the room.

The new boy jumped to his feet and smiled broadly, revealing a gap in his lower front teeth. "I am being happy to know American school," he said, his words thickly accented. Several children laughed.

"Josephat is learning English," smiled Ms. Bartels, "so be sure to help him. Ernesto, would you like to find Tanzania on the map and show the rest of us where it is?"

While Ernesto studied the big world map on the wall, two dozen pairs of eyes studied Josephat. Randy tried to figure out what was different about him. At least half the class was African-American, so it wasn't his skin color. Maybe it was the way he sat so straight, and the way he kept smiling. His clothing was like the other boys, but his hair was shaved close to his head. Then Randy saw the circles. A small round mark, like the imprint from a bottle cap, high on each cheek. Randy wondered why a kid would paint circles on his face.

During recess, Randy and two friends checked out a soccer ball and practiced kicks and fancy footwork on the grass. Their breathless attempts to outdo each other were interrupted by loud laughter coming from the lunch tables a few yards away. Curious, they stopped their game and moved in that direction.

Several children were gathered around Josephat. Some were laughing and pointing. Others were huddled together whispering and giggling. Josephat, smiling as always, looked confused. The empty space between his teeth made him look a little dumb, too, Randy thought.

Gary, a big sixth-grader who was always acting smart, said to the group, "He gave me most of his lunch! Half the sandwich, the apple, most of the cookies. Every time he pulled something out of the bag, he handed it to me. Then he acted like I was supposed to give him my lunch. I guess he thought we were having a picnic!" Gary doubled over laughing.

Randy thought about tolerance. He remembered what his mother said and what he was learning in Mrs. Bartels class. Randy took a deep breath and yelled to Gary and anyone else who was listening, "Leave Josephat alone. So what if he thought it was a picnic? Maybe they have picnics in Africa."

Seconds later, the bell rang. Children quickly forgot about Josephat and headed for their classrooms. Randy walked silently beside Josephat. Out of the corner of his eye, he studied the circle on Josephat's left cheek. It wasn't painted on; it was part of Josephat's skin. "A scar," Randy thought.

All afternoon, and for the next two days, Josephat kept the kids in Randy's class amused. Every time Ms. Bartels called on him or even mentioned his name, Josephat jumped to his feet, grinning. Twice Randy laughed with the other kids and then felt guilty. The first time Ms. Bartels asked Josephat to help pass out some papers, he answered very seriously, "Yes, Mama." All the kids looked at each other in disbelief, then burst out laughing. For the rest of the day, Ms. Bartels was "Mama" to some of the class clowns. "Yes Mama" this, and "Yes Mama" that.

Josephat's English was slow and oddly phrased. Randy could see smirks and hear giggles every time Josephat spoke. Two boys in the back of the room made a game of imitating Josephat's stiff posture.

All the while Tolerance in big black bulletin-board letters loomed over the class. Like the giant oak tree in front of the school, Tolerance was part of the scenery — so nobody saw it.

On Sunday afternoon, Duane and Michael came over. They played computer games and rode their bikes to the park where they sat on the grass and talked about summer vacation.

"If you could do anything you wanted this summer, what would you choose?" asked Randy.

Duane thought a minute. "I'd go on one of those cruises," he said. "My cousin went on a Caribbean cruise and ended up with three days at Disney World. That'd be cool."

"What about you, Michael?" asked Randy.

"I'd go visit my grandfather in Idaho and go fishing," answered Michael. "Gramps knows all the best rivers and camping spots."

"If I could do anything," said Randy, "I'd work at the zoo this summer. Sometimes they let kids have jobs as keeper's aides."

"That's a stupid idea," said Duane. "If you could do anything you wanted, why stay here? You're here all year long. Go to Hawaii or Paris or China."

"It's not a stupid idea," said Randy. "I want to learn about animals."

"But that's like school," said Michael. "You probably get graded and everything. Duane's right. Do something fun, not something nerdy."

"Randy's always a nerd," said Duane. "He doesn't know what fun is."

"Oh yeah, why'd you come over today then?" asked Randy. "If I'm so boring, why come to my house at all?"

"Because I couldn't think of anything better to do, that's why," said Duane. "Com'on Mike, let's go. I don't want to keep 'Randa-the-Panda' from dreaming about the zoo."

As Randy rode his bike home, he thought about what his friends had said. He really did want to work at the zoo. He had a right to his own idea of fun. Duane and Michael were just being selfish. They were being…

"Intolerant," Randy said out loud. The word popped out from some corner of his brain, surprising him and causing him to swerve sharply. He had just rounded the corner in front of the Stewart's house, and a friendly voice called out, "Hey, slow down Randy! It's not even dinner time!"

It was Mr. Stewart working inside his open garage. Randy was embarrassed. He must have been riding faster than he realized. He pulled his bike around and stopped. Getting off, he let the bike drop gently on the front lawn. "Sorry, Mr. Stewart," Randy said, walking into the garage.

"You must have been thinking hard about something," laughed Mr. Stewart. "You've met Josephat, haven't you?"

It was then that Randy saw Josephat, sitting on a stool near the back of the garage. Josephat smiled and stood up. Randy said hello. He couldn't think of anything else to say, and the two boys just stood there looking at each other self-consciously.

After a moment, Mr. Stewart looked around from his workbench. "Josephat, why don't you take Randy inside and get him a glass of water."

"Oh, no thanks," said Randy quickly. "I'd better be getting home."

"What's the hurry?" asked Mr. Stewart. "Like I said, it's not even dinner time. And besides, Josephat needs the practice." Mr. Stewart winked at Randy, making it impossible for him to leave.

Josephat poured two glasses of water and gave one to Randy, who drank it thirstily. "Thanks," Randy said, setting the empty glass on the counter. He looked at Josephat and felt stupidly speechless. Finally, he asked, "Want to show me your room?"

"My room?" repeated Josephat. "Oh, yes. Come."

Josephat's small room had what looked to Randy like African pictures on the walls, along with framed photographs of people in large and small groups. Josephat explained that these were school friends in Tanzania. Carved animals sat in groups on the dresser, bookcase, and bedside table. "Wow," said Randy, picking up a painted wood giraffe.

"You like the giraffe? Please, you must have it," said Josephat.

"No, no," Randy said politely. "It's yours. Randy's finger traced the smooth surface of a carved elephant.

"Then take elephant," insisted Josephat.

Every time Randy saw something he liked, Josephat tried to give it to him. Randy stopped admiring Josephat's things, and instead looked at Josephat. His eyes went to the circles on Josephat's cheeks.

"All boys have," explained Josephat. "In Maasai tribe, a sign of beauty," he said. He pointed to his cheeks and said, "Only boys." Then he pointed to the gap where his lower front tooth had been cut out, saying, "Girls, too." Josephat laughed and said, "I must get a tooth for America. Not beautiful here."

Josephat and Randy both laughed.

On Monday morning, Ms. Bartels pointed to the word Tolerance on the bulletin board. She asked children to reflect on what they learned about tolerance during the past week. She told them to write about what tolerance meant to them, and then she asked volunteers to read what they had written. Randy raised his hand. When Ms. Bartels called on him, he read:

"Tolerance is when it's okay for your friend to spend his summer doing something that he thinks is fun — even if you don't think it's fun."

"Tolerance is accepting others just as they are even when they look different or have different ideas or different ways of doing things."

When the noon bell rang, Randy took his lunch and went outside. He found Josephat sitting at a lunch table and scooted in next to him. Randy opened his lunch. He took out a sandwich, grapes, carrot sticks, and cookies. He spread everything out on the table. Josephat did the same. Then Randy gave half of everything he had to Josephat who, laughing, did the same in return.

When other kids walked by, Randy said, "Josephat and I are having a picnic. Want to join us? Several children did.

Questions for Discussion and Reflection:

1. Why did the other children make fun of Josephat?
2. How was Josephat different from the other children? How was he the same?
3. How do you think Josephat felt as a new child in a strange country?
4. What does it mean to recognize the beliefs and practices of another person?
5. Does recognizing and accepting a person's beliefs and practices mean that you have to agree with them or make them your own? Explain.

Randy Learns About Tolerance
Reflection Sheet

Randy's teacher told children to think about what tolerance meant to them. Here's a place to write about what tolerance means to you:

2. Has anyone ever been intolerant of you or something about you? What happened and how did you feel?

1. Why do you think it is important to be tolerant of people who have different beliefs and customs than you have?

3. When have you demonstrated tolerance for someone or something?

Meet Pebble Pete

An Experiment in the Recognition of Unique Characteristics

This activity teaches children to:

— describe the unique characteristics of one member of a group of similar objects.
— compare the stereotyping of objects to the stereotyping of people.
— explain that it is the responsibility of the viewer to differentiate one person from another.

You will need:

a paper bag containing a collection of small rocks or pebbles, all very similar in size, shape, and color (apples, oranges, potatoes, or nuts may be substituted)

Directions:

Begin by asking: *Have you ever noticed how people tend to generalize about other people? By "generalize," I mean lump people together in groups. When we group people or things together and consider that they are all the same, it's called stereotyping. We usually only do that with people we don't know very well. It's hard to stereotype a friend.*

Open the paper bag and show the pebbles (or the items you have chosen) to your child/children. In your own words, say:

These pebbles all look pretty much the same at first glance. But that's because you don't know them. Therefore, I'm going to give you an opportunity to meet and become acquainted with one of these pebbles.

Pass the bag full of pebbles and have your child/children reach in and take one. Also choose a pebble for yourself. Direct your child/children to take 1 minute to examine their pebble very carefully — to notice its features and everything unique about it well enough that they would be able to introduce it to others. After 1 minute, begin the sharing by introducing your own pebble. For example, say something like:

This is Pebble Pete. Pete began his life on a mountainside. When he was first chipped from his mother, who was a big boulder, he hit the ground and kept sliding — right down the mountain! That experience scratched him up quite a bit. During his first winter, he was washed into a river and spent almost four years traveling downstream. The water smoothed him out, but I can still see one or two scratches on this side. Finally Pete came ashore near the wide mouth of the river and was eventually scooped up by a man who collected pebbles in his pickup truck and sold them to the landscapers and nurseries in town. That's how I met Pebble Pete. Now he has a job on a pathway in the garden.

Invite your child/children to introduce their pebbles in the same way by creating a story about the pebble based on its appearance and giving it a name. Next, instruct them to return their pebble to the paper bag. Be sure you remove any extra pebbles from the bag before you collect, or if working with one child, leave some peblles in the bag.

In your own words ask: *Now that you and your pebble have become friends, do you think that it will still look just like all the other pebbles? Let's find out. I'm going to pour all the pebbles out so that you can find yours and take it back.*

Roll the pebbles out of the bag onto the floor. Have your child/children examine all the pebbles, identify the one they had, and to keep their pebble "friend". Have them explain why they know they have identified their special pebble while focusing on the idea that everyone has individual characteristics and that stereotyping is a belief that is limiting to everyone.

Conclude the activity with a discussion.

Questions for Discussion and Reflection:

1. Have you ever heard someone say, "They're all alike"? What will you think the next time you hear that expression?
2. Why do people lump others into groups and pretend they are all alike?
3. What can you say or do if you hear someone stereotyping a person based on color, sex, religion, or some other characteristic?
4. Whose job is it to see and acknowledge the differences between one person and another?

Extension:

Allow your child/children to decorate their pebbles with miniature designs. They can apply opaque paints with the tips of small brushes or with Q-tips. Ask them to choose colors and designs that they feel could represent the "history" they have created for their pebbles.

If the Shoe Fits
An Experiment in Categorizing

This activity teaches children to:

— categorize objects according to a variety of criteria.
— explain that a category both includes and excludes members.
— list categories into which we routinely group people.
— discuss the benefits and drawbacks of categorizing people.

You will need:

a variety of single shoes — old, new, dress, casual, sandals, sneakers, child's, adult's, representing a variety of colors, sizes, styles and heel heights (the more samples, the better); instead of real shoes, you could provide pictures of shoes from catalogs and advertisements; the internet is also a rich source for shoe photos and illustrations

Directions:

Spread the shoes or pictures of shoes out on the floor.

Ask your child/children to look at the shoes and come up with suitable categories for grouping the shoes. (In addition to the categories mentioned under "You will need:" you might have shoes that are athletic, hiking, formal, orthopedic, rain, snow, etc.)

Next, see if the categories can be paired up. For example:

child _____ adult
dress _____ casual
old _____ new
leather _____ fabric
high heel _____ low heel
open _____ closed

Taking one set of categories at a time, have your child/children physically arrange the shoes into the two groups using as many shoes as possible.

Ask them to notice:
— Which shoes don't seem to fit either category and are therefore "left out" after each grouping.
— Which shoes fit the most categories and which the fewest.
— Which categories are more inclusive and which are less.
— Which categories seem better than others and why.
— How they decide where to put a shoe when it fits two categories equally.
— If they try to bend or stretch a category so that a shoe fits.

Talk about the purpose of having categories and groups. Who is helped by grouping and labeling shoes? Point out that whenever a category is created to include certain items, it automatically excludes others. In a culminating discussion, turn the attention of your child/children from shoes to people, and examine how these concepts and insights apply to the categorizing of people, too. Brainstorm and list all the different people categories that they can think of. Refer to the list throughout the discussion.

Questions for Discussion and Reflection:

1. How do we categorize people?
2. Who is helped by categorizing people?
3. What groups of people have not been accepted by the dominant culture during our history? How were they treated?
4. How do you feel when you are excluded (left out)?
5. How do groups of people feel when the culture excludes or limits them? What do they do?

A Friend I Have Who Is Different From Me

A Sharing Circle

This Sharing Circle teaches children to:

— demonstrate that friendships form across racial, cultural, and other types of boundaries.
— describe the relative importance of commonalties and differences in a friendship.

Introduce the Topic:

Today we're going to talk about our friends, particularly the ones who are different from us in some significant way. Our topic is, "A Friend I Have Who Is Different From Me."

Tell us about a friend of yours who is either much older or much younger, is of a different race or culture, or is very different from you in some other way. Tell us how you became friends with this person and what you like about them. I'll give you a few moments to decide what you want to share. Our topic is, "A Friend I Have Who Is Different From Me."

Questions for Discussion and Reflection:

1. What were the reasons you gave for liking your friends and valuing their friendship?
2. What, if any, problems or conflicts have been caused by the difference between you and your friend, and how have you handled them?
3. What have you and your friend been able to learn from each other as a result of your differences?
4. What is more important between friends, the things you have in common or your differences? Why?

A Way I Show Tolerance
A Sharing Circle

This Sharing Circle teaches children to:

— describe examples of tolerant behavior.
— recognize that a multicultural society includes people of different beliefs who have different ways of doing things.

Introduce the Topic:

Tolerance is a very important word in our language. It also conveys a very important idea. Tolerance means recognizing and accepting the beliefs and practices of others, especially when they are different from our own. Today, we're going to talk about what it means to recognize and accept another person's beliefs and ways of doing things. Our topic is, "A Way I Show Tolerance."

How do you show your friends, classmates and family member that it's okay with you if they have different beliefs than you have, and do things in different ways? When someone says something you don't agree with, do you listen carefully and see what you can learn? Maybe you say something like, "That's your opinion, but I have a different one," or "That's interesting," or "Let me see if I understand you." Or perhaps you just remain quiet and don't say anything. Think about this carefully. Our topic is, "A Way I Show Tolerance."

Questions for Discussion and Reflection:

1. Can you think of anything you do every day that couldn't be done in a different way?
2. Why do people get into arguments and fights over the "right" answer or the "right" way of doing something?
3. Why is it important to show tolerance for the beliefs and practices of others?

What Did You Learn About Tolerance?

Use this page to think about and record the things you have learned about tolerance. You can write, draw pictures, scribble and doodle, create a poem, or anything else that has meaning to you and will help you remember what you have learned.

When you finish, show this page to someone else and explain what you have learned.

SERVICE TO OTHERS

"An essential part of a happy, healthy life is being of service to others."

Sue Patton Thoele

Tips for Teaching Service to Others:

Create a family scrapbook of Service to Others. Use pictures in your album, add notes about the services performed, brochures where the service took place, thank you notes and anything else that is meaningful.

———————

Be an example yourself. If an elderly neighbor needs help with cleaning his yard, help him out. If someone with a handful of papers drops them, help in picking them up. Lead by what you do.

———————

Make it a family tradition to discuss at the dinner table how you helped someone out that day. Let your child brag about what was done and make sure you praise your child for all good acts, big or small.

———————

Ask your child to make a list of things he or she is grateful for. When you discuss the list, point out which items other boys and girls don't have. Help your child to feel special and grateful, and encourage him or her to help others who have much less.

Vocabulary Words

- Invention
- Blurted
- Materializing
- Commotion
- Haste
- Volunteered

Marvin's Last Invention

Marvin was always inventing something strange.

Once he invented a bubble gum that lasted four days without losing its flavor. Another time he invented a machine that let you eat dinner, listen to your parents and do your homework all at once so you'd have more time to play.

Half of what he invented never worked, and most of the kids thought he was crazy. But this, he thought, was his best invention yet — the "Deluxe Wish-A-World."

The Wish-A-World was secretly hooked up to his dad's computer. Marvin entered the name of any book on his dad's bookshelf and a page number, and one day later, whatever object or topic was being discussed on that page, anywhere in the world, would appear.

He tested it with the book How Things Work, page 46, about how pencils are made. In the morning his dad's desk was stuffed with bright new yellow unsharpened pencils — enough for all the people living on his block!

"Wonderful!" he blurted out in the middle of breakfast. Marvin could hardly believe it! Fortunately, no one paid any attention because everyone had come to accept Marvin's outbursts of strange behavior as normal for someone who seemed to spend as much time daydreaming as Marvin.

Marvin quickly got the encyclopedia and turned to "G." He was going to become rich overnight by materializing "gold." He hastily typed in the encyclopedia's name, volume number 7 and page 314, and set the machine to work. That night he hardly slept, bursting with excitement.

When Marvin woke up the next day, there was a giant commotion. Police cars, and ambulances were lined up and down the street. Paramedics, the Red Cross, doctors, nurses, and scores of other people were rushing in and out of all the homes and spilling out into the yards. He thought there had been some sort of accident until he got closer and saw that inside all the houses were hundreds and hundreds of children from all over the world, dressed in every kind of clothing imaginable and speaking different languages. It was mass confusion!

In his haste to enter his request for "gold" Marvin had left out a digit in the page number. Instead of reading 314, it read 34, the page for "Children." There were so many children in the neighborhood that there was no room to walk! And the worst part of it was that over half of them were either starving or sick.

Teams of parents and community volunteers had been called to bring in food and water. Most of the hungry children were not even five-years old. Nurses were there to give them shots because many of children were sick with diseases that kids in the United States rarely got anymore, and if they didn't get treatment fast, some were going to die!

Marvin was white as a sheet with fright! What had he done? After he figured out that his machine was somehow responsible for the mess, he thought of telling his mother, but got scared when he heard the chief of police shout, "Who's responsible for this? They're in big trouble!"

The sick and hungry children were from the poor countries that made up over half of the world. Some of their homes had been bombed in wars. Others were poor because pollution or lack of rain had made it impossible for their families to grow food. And still others were from overcrowded cities where they had been sleeping in the street and begging.

It was pitiful and Marvin felt sick. Not only had he created problems for his community, but the needs of these children seemed impossible to meet. And how would he ever send them back! The machine was only for getting things, not giving them back. Marvin thought he would be locked up for the next 100 years!

But as he watched, a strange thing happened. After the initial shock, people seemed to be happily working together. For all the trouble they went through to get food, medicine, and clothing for children, they were enjoying themselves! And no one seemed mad! In fact, someone said, "We've got more than enough here. I'm glad these children can use it."

Marvin woke with a start. "What a dream!" he said to himself. He got dressed and ran out into the street without even having breakfast. As soon as he saw the street was empty, he dashed back into the house and turned off his machine. Luckily, he stopped it before anything appeared.

At breakfast that morning Marvin said, "I've got a great idea. "Why don't we make a project of studying how children live in other countries and maybe even raise some money to send them so they won't be so hungry!"

His family was stunned. Not only did Marvin rarely speak, he almost never made sense when he did.

"Good idea!" said his mother with a puzzled look on her face. Everyone else agreed too.

Marvin's "Deluxe Wish-A-World" machine never did work after that, but he didn't care. Marvin got so involved in the project that he forgot about inventing crazy things. Instead, he invented more ways to help children all over the world get what they wished for.

Questions for Discussion and Reflection:

1. Why did Marvin turn off the machine before the gold appeared?
2. Why were most of the children hungry or sick? Name some of the countries the children may have come from.
3. Why didn't Marvin invent any more crazy things?
4. What made Marvin's family decide to accept Marvin's idea to study about and help children?
5. Why is it important to help others?
6. What are some ways that people can be of service to our community? ...to the nation? ...the world?
7. What would things be like if no one helped anyone else?

Marvin's Last Invention
Reflection Sheet

Think about the story of Marvin, his inventions, and his dream. Then answer these questions:

1. What did Marvin realize about children of the world when he saw them in his dream? What made him want to help them?

3. How do you benefit personally from being of service to others? What do you get out of it?

2. Think of a time when you performed some kind of service for another person, a group, or the community. It could have been something as small as picking up some litter, or it could have been a major project. What did you do and how did you feel about it?

No More Litter
An Environmental Awareness Activity

This activity teaches children to:

— develop and present anti-littering posters
— explain that littering can be reduced through awareness of the problem and taking steps to prevent it
— state that litter is unsightly, dangerous and is costly to clean up

You will need:

poster-size art paper, magic markers, assorted art supplies such as colored paper; cloth; glue; optional litter items such as styrofoam cups, cigarette butts, candy wrappers, plastic bags, 6-pack rings, etc.

Directions:

Develop interest in the topic of litter by asking your child/children, *What's wrong with litter?* Listen to the responses, and use their comments to lead a discussion incorporating the following points:

- Litter is illegal. Litter is dirty. Not only does it look ugly but it can carry germs. Some animals are attracted to litter and pick up germs from it, and they can get sick or carry the germs to people.

- Litter is bad for the environment. It can get washed down into storm drains and be carried into rivers and lakes and oceans. Sometimes litter is dumped directly into water where it can be dangerous to birds and fish. The water can also become polluted and no longer safely be used for drinking and recreation.

- Litter also costs lots of money to clean up and when cans and bottles are not recycled, more resources and money must be used to create cans and bottles from new resources.

If computers are available have your child/children extend their knowledge of the problem of littering by doing internet research.

Direct your child/children to select either a problem that littering causes or a remedy of what they should do with trash. Say to them: *Learn as much as you can about littering, then create a poster that shows either a problem that littering causes or a solution to the problem of littering. See how clearly and cleverly you can get your point across. Do this by combining words and illustrations. Use any of the art materials provided.* Tell your child/children how long you will give them to create their posters and when they will present and explain their posters to you and others in your group or to other family members.

Make the art materials available and encourage your child/children to add their own embellishments, including the "litter items". Answer questions and help as needed. If you are home schooling more than one child, encourage discussion and collaboration.

When the posters have been completed, have your child/children prepare a brief presentation to show their poster and to tell about it.

After the posters have been completed, discuss their reactions to the information gained. Ask these and your own discussion questions.

Questions for Discussion and Reflection:

1. What has been the most interesting or surprising thing you've learned about the problem of littering?
2. How can each of us prevent littering?
3. How does littering affect many more people than just the person who litters?
4. How are we being of service to others when we don't litter or when we take the time to pick up litter we come across?

Extension:

Plan a litter pickup activity as a family or a learning group. Determine a time and place to collect litter such as a park or safe roadside. Bring garbage bags and protective gloves or tongs. When the litter has been gathered, recycle as much as possible. Make it a challenge for your child/children to learn what can and cannot be recycled.

Making Community Gift Basket

A Community Service Activity

This activity teaches children to:

— identify the needs of local agencies.
— create and assemble gifts for others.

You will need:

a variety of gift items; suitable containers; wrapping and decorating materials

Directions:

Choose an appropriate local agency for which your child/children can make gift baskets. It might be a day-care facility, senior center, assisted-living home, or animal rescue agency. Preferably pick an organization that is local and for which it is possible for your child/children to do some research. Depending on the chosen agency, have your child/children find out such things as:

— the number of residents (children, seniors, animals)
— needs of the agency (Animal agencies might need old towels and blankets and donations of animal food. Day-care facilities may like gently used story books. Senior centers might be happy to have children create letters and cards for each resident or come in and read to their residents.)
— whether the organization would welcome gifts (and perhaps visits) from children
— the best times of the day for visits

As a group, choose the organization and determine what kinds of "gifts" your child/children would like to provide. Determine if it is best to prepare one large gift basket or several smaller or individual baskets for the organization. Decide what kind of container will best hold the contents of the gift baskets. You may use actual baskets or you may find that boxes, gift bags, or bags that your child/children decorate themselves work better.

Brainstorm with your child/children how they can collect the items for the baskets. Some ideas might be to circulate a flyer describing the project and listing needed items. Perhaps your child/children would like to hold a fund-raiser (bake sale, car wash, lemon aide stand, etc.) to raise money to buy the items for the baskets. The basket items might include things belonging to your child/children that they can donate such as story books for young children.

Have your child/children assemble the gift baskets and wrap or decorate them. Determine the best way to deliver the baskets.

If an actual visit is possible, talk to the organization to find out what other activities your child/children can engage in during their visit. For example, they might:

— perform a skit
— lead some sing-a-longs
— play games
— lead simple stretching and movement exercises
— teach the young children or seniors a dance (wheelchairs can dance, too)

Prepare and practice with your child/children whatever activity it is that is planned, and discuss appropriate behavior.

After the baskets are delivered or the visit has been made, lead a follow-up discussion.

Questions for Discussion and Reflection:

1. What was the best part of this activity for you?
2. How did making the gift basket cause you to feel?
3. How do you think the recipients of the gift baskets felt?
4. Would you like to do something like this again? What ideas do you have for another visit or gift basket? Who would you like give it to (or visit) next time?

Something Nice I Did for a Friend

A Sharing Circle

This Sharing Circle teaches children to:

— describe ways of being of service to others.
— discuss how thoughtful deeds benefit both giver and receiver.

Introduce the Topic:

Our topic for this session is, "Something Nice I Did for a Friend." Friends do thoughtful things for each other all the time. That's part of what builds friendship. Tell us something that you did for one of your friends. It doesn't have to be something spectacular — small deeds are important, too. For example, maybe you accompanied your friend to the library and helped her find some books for a report. Perhaps you offered to feed your friend's pet while he was on vacation. Or maybe you were a good listener when your friend was feeling sad or upset about something. Have you ever drawn a picture or made a little gift for a friend? Have you ever given a friend a funny card? There are many thoughtful things we can do for our friends. Tell us about one. The topic is, "Something Nice I Did for a Friend."

Questions for Discussion and Reflection:

1. How do you feel when you help someone else?
2. Does it matter if the help is a big thing or a little thing?
3. How does the other person feel when you help them?

What I Wish I Could Do to Make This a Better World

A Sharing Circle

This Sharing Circle teaches children to:

— identify global problems that need to be addressed.
— explain their relationship to the planet and all its people.

Introduce the Topic:

Our topic today allows us to think big and not worry about whether or not something is truly possible. We're going to talk about the way we <u>wish</u> things could be. The topic is, "What I Wish I Could Do to Make This a Better World."

If you could do anything you wished to make this a better world, what would it be? What would you give to the whole world? Maybe you'd give every kid a happy home with a loving family. Or maybe you'd send food to all the people who are hungry. Perhaps you'd give all people a good education so that they could be productive and successful. Maybe you'd make the world a better place by getting rid of pollution, or showing people how to settle conflicts peacefully, or giving everyone the ability to speak and understand many languages so they could communicate better. Or you might choose to make the world a better place by doing something fun. Use your imagination and tell us what you would do. The topic is, "What I Wish I Could Do to Make This a Better World."

Questions for Discussion and Reflection:

1. Which of our ideas might really be possible? How might they be accomplished?
2. Why is it important to think about the well being of the whole world? Why can't we just worry about ourselves?
3. What are some things that we can do to make the world a better place?

What Did You Learn About Service to Others?

Use this page to think about and record the things you have learned about service to others. You can write, draw pictures, scribble and doodle, create a poem, or anything else that has meaning to you and will help you remember what you have learned.

When you finish, show this page to someone else and explain what you have learned.

RESPONSIBILITY

"People need responsibility. They resist assuming it, but they cannot get along without it."

John Steinbeck

Tips for Teaching Responsibility:

We all want our children to act responsibly because they want to, not just because they are told to. Explain how a football team (or any team) needs more than one great player to win games. In the same way your family needs everyone's contribution to run smoothly and well. Talk about the various roles each family member plays and how everyone's help and contribution is important. Be sure to praise your child for being responsible and for doing his or her part in the family.

Age-appropriate chores are a simple way to teach your child responsibility, and letting your child make some of his or her own choices will help teach responsibility and accountability.

Being a responsible adult sets a good example for your child's watchful eyes. Following through with what you say, keeping a promise, or being on time are ways you can set good examples.

Vocabulary Words

- Stooped
- Excitedly
- Chatted
- Pretending
- Confrontation
- Flickered
- Fitfully
- Sheepishly

Anna and the Silver Bracelet

"Hurry up, Lynette," said Anna impatiently. "We'll be late getting home."

"Okay, okay," replied Lynette, as she stooped over to pick something off the ground in front of the Smith house.

Anna turned expecting Lynette to be right behind her. But instead she heard Lynette cry out, "Wow! Come look at this, Anna!"

Anna sighed and retraced her steps. Lynette was just getting to her feet when she said "Look what I found. It was laying on the ground," she exclaimed excitedly. She held up something shiny and silver. Anna couldn't tell what it was.

"Great," said Anna. "I'm going home. Mom will have dinner ready and I'm supposed to be home on time to eat." With that she started home at top speed. Lynette had to run to catch up.

"Isn't it beautiful?" Lynette said, admiring the silver thing in her hand.

"What is it?" asked Anna. She was more interested in reaching home than looking at Lynette's treasure.

"A bracelet, silly. I think it's real silver."

"I wonder who lost it," said Anna. "The Smiths had a party last night and there were lots of people there. Maybe one of their guests lost it."

Anna could hear her mother call everyone to dinner just as she turned the knob. Lynette continued up the hill to her house while Anna watched her quickly shove the silver bracelet into a jeans pocket. Anna was surprised. She knew Lynette had been taught to try to find the owner of lost items, just as she had. Anna figured that there was a pretty good chance that someone at the Smith's party had lost it. Oh well, thought Anna, Lynette was probably waiting till later.

The next day Jeff was walking with Anna and Lynette. He kept the girls in stitches with funny stories about the new puppies at his house. His mother was a breeder of cocker spaniels, so daily Jeff had some new mischief to report.

As soon as Jeff turned down Tower Street and the two girls were climbing the hill to their own block, Lynette withdrew the silver bracelet from her pocket. She held it up so the sun reflected off the smooth metal. Then she let it slip down over her wrist and admired it against her skin.

"Did you go to the Smith's to see if someone from their party had lost the bracelet?" asked Anna, trying not to sound accusing.

"Oh, not yet. I just forgot, I guess," said Lynette dreamily. A moment later she added, "But I will," before dropping the bracelet into her pocket.

As always, they reached Anna's house first. Anna trudged up the walk and turned at the door to wave and watch as Lynette climbed the hill to her own home at the end of the street.

The next afternoon, while Anna and Lynette were hanging out at Anna's house Mrs. Smith called Anna's mother to inquire if Anna, or any of the other kids who walked up and down the street, had found a silver bracelet. Mrs. Smith explained that the bracelet had been lost by a guest who was at their party on Saturday, and it was very important and meaningful to the person who lost it. Anna's mother told the girls about the call and asked them to let Mrs. Smith know if they learn anything about the bracelet.

Anna shot a questioning look at Lynette who immediately looked down at the floor and said she had to go home. Lynette left without looking up. Anna wanted to talk to Lynette about the bracelet but she never had a chance. Lynette was gone in a second and didn't call that night as she usually did.

Anna had trouble concentrating on anything. Images of the shiny silver bracelet kept popping into her mind. Mostly she thought about the bracelet on her friend's wrist. Lynette loved jewelry and it was easy to see she was crazy about that bracelet. Was she planning to keep it?

Anna decided to find out. Feeling nervous but determined, she picked up her phone and called Lynette. When Lynette answered, she sounded breathless and cheerful. "Hi, sorry I forgot to call you last night. I was watching a movie with my brother and when it was over it was too late."

The girls got right into talking about their friends and boys and family outings. Finally Anna remembered why she called and asked, "Lynette, have you talked to Mrs. Smith about the bracelet?"

Silence.

"Lynette? Are you there?"

Finally, her voice shaking, Lynette said slowly, "Anna, I told you I wasn't going to keep it. Just don't bug me about it, okay?"

"But have you talked to her?" persisted Anna.

"No, not yet. I keep forgetting. What's the matter, don't you trust me? Anyway, it's none of your business!" Now Lynette's voice sounded angry.

"But it doesn't belong to you Lynette, and somebody feels bad because it's gone. How would you feel if..."

Anna realized that Lynette had hung up. She felt awful and wondered if she was being a bad friend. She thought about calling Lynette back and apologizing, but decided against it. Maybe she should just mind her own business.

But minding her own business was tough for Anna. Especially when "lost bracelet" posters began to show up around the neighborhood. She saw one on a bulletin board outside the grocery store and another taped to the side of the post office. She practically ran into one stapled to a utility pole on the edge of the park.

The more she thought about it, the more Anna realized that the lost bracelet was her business. After all, she was there when Lynette found it. She saw Lynette admire it on her wrist and put the bracelet in her pocket. And Lynette was her best friend — though, come to think of it, she wasn't acting very friendly these days.

A couple of afternoons later, Anna and Lynette were at the park playing on the bars with several other girls, when someone mentioned the lost bracelet.

"My mom won't let me wear my nice stuff just everyday" said one girl, "It's too easy to lose."

"Yea, and who's going to turn in a bracelet like that? Most kids would keep it," said another.

"Finders keepers, losers weepers," chanted Lynette. The other girls laughed.

Anna couldn't believe her ears. Lynette really did plan to keep the bracelet, and not only that — she thought it was okay! Right then and there, Anna made up her mind to visit Mrs. Elliott.

Mrs. Elliott was one of Anna's favorite people. She was a neighbor, went to the same church and had been Anna's babysitter when she was younger. She was always friendly and helpful. Anna and Mrs. Elliott often talked, sometimes taking long walks around the neighborhood. Anna felt she could always go to Mrs. Elliott with her problems.

When Anna knocked on her door, Ms. Elliott opened it and smiled brightly. "Hi, Anna," she said. "Come in and sit down. I haven't had a visit from you in a while. Why don't you bring me up to date."

They chatted about things Anna had been up to and about Anna's family. Anna felt nervous and the pleasant conversation calmed her. After a few minutes, Ms. Elliott paused and asked, "Did you have a special reason for dropping by today, Anna?" Anna nodded and stared at the floor. Ms. Elliott waited.

Finally, Anna blurted out, "I know who has the lost bracelet. I saw her pick it up off the ground in front of the Smith's house and put in her pocket. I don't think she's going to return it."

Anna told Ms. Elliott the whole story. She explained that keeping the secret was making her feel bad, and she expressed her confusion over what to do. She wanted to be loyal to her best friend, but didn't think it was right for Lynette to keep something that didn't belong to her. Ms. Elliott listened. She let Anna know that she understood how hard it was to tell on a friend. In the end, though, Ms. Elliott stressed that Anna was feeling badly because she was going against her own conscience.

"Pretending you don't know anything about the bracelet is not a responsible thing to do," said Ms. Elliott seriously. "Your conscience won't let you be like an ostrich who sticks her head in the sand. It wants you to be a responsible person, and there are only two ways to do that. Either convince Lynette that she must return the bracelet, or report what you know."

"But Lynette will hate me," worried Anna.

"Maybe not," said Ms. Elliott. "You don't know how Lynette really feels about keeping the bracelet. I'll bet that deep down, she has just as many doubts as you."

Anna felt better when she left Ms. Elliott's home. She decided to try that afternoon, one more time, to talk some sense into Lynette.

Later that day the two girls were climbing the hill toward home. Anna wanted to talk about the bracelet but didn't know how to begin her confrontation, so she said instead, "That's a cool jacket, Lynette. Is it new?"

"Isn't it great! My dad bought it for me on a business trip. Everybody kept coming up to me all day, telling me how much they liked it. It's the neatest jacket I've ever had!" exclaimed Lynette, proudly.

A little light bulb flickered in Anna's brain. "You probably shouldn't wear it when you go out" she said, watching Lynette's reaction.

"Why not? shrugged Lynette, "It's been cold lately."

Anna focused on the sidewalk and tried to speak casually. "Because if you ever lay it on a bench, or hang it over the back of a chair, or leave it on a hook someplace, you'll probably never see it again."

Lynette's steps slowed, but she didn't say anything, so Anna plunged ahead.

"Whoever finds it will think it's cool and keep it," she said.

"They wouldn't do that," protested Lynette.

"Sure they will. They'll say 'finders keepers' and they won't worry about you at all," insisted Anna.

Suddenly Lynette stopped. "I know why you're saying this to me, Anna, and it's a mean thing to do. You're hoping someone will take my jacket because of the bracelet. If you care so much about that old bracelet, why don't you find out who lost it and be her friend! I don't want you for a friend anymore!"

Anna stood alone at her front gate, watching Lynette storm up the hill. She felt sad and fought the urge to cry.

The sadness grew as afternoon turned to evening and smells of dinner drifted through the house. Anna wasn't hungry. She knew she was going to have to tell on Lynette and it made her feel queasy. She picked her way through the meal, trying to act normal and she slept fitfully that night

Anna didn't expect to see Lynette the next morning, so she was surprised when her "ex-friend" showed up at the front gate. Nervously, Anna walked to the gate. "Hi," she said. "I didn't think you'd want to get together today." Anna noticed that Lynette was not wearing her new jacket. She was wearing the silver bracelet.

"I'm sorry about yesterday," said Lynette sheepishly. "I thought about what you said all night. I realized that if someone found my jacket and kept it, I'd think they were the worst person in the world. The more I thought about it, the more I felt like the worst person in the world."

Anna was so relieved her knees started to shake.

Lynette took off the bracelet and held it out to Anna. "Here," she said. "Take it. I never really wanted it. ...Well, maybe I did at first, but not for long. Will you take it to Mrs. Smith for me?"

Anna shook her head firmly. "No, Lynette," she said, "you have to do it. You were the one who found it and you were the one who kept it all this time, so you're the one who has to turn it in."

"But I'm scared," pleaded Lynette. "That's why I didn't take it back. I was just admiring it in my drawer, and I kept putting it off. Then after a few days I couldn't take it back because it would look like I was planning to keep it. It's really stupid, but I don't know how to explain it!"

"You can say exactly what you said to me," suggested Anna. "I talked to Mrs. Elliott about it, and she said we'll feel better if we take responsibility for our actions. I think she's right."

"We?" questioned Lynette.

"Yes, we," repeated Anna. "I knew you had the bracelet all this time, and I didn't say anything until I talked to Ms. Elliott. Of course, she didn't tell on us. She just put it back on me. So I have to go with you and take responsibility for playing dumb."

"Really? You'll go with me?" said Lynette hopefully.

"Sure," said Anna. "You'll see, — it won't be so bad. Wait while I get my things and we'll go do it right now."

Anna ran in the house and was back in less than two minutes, breathlessly stumbling through the gate. The two friends threw their arms around each other and hugged. Laughing, they headed down the hill to the Smith house.

"Come on," said Lynette. "Let's get this over with!"

Questions for Discussion and Reflection:

1. What's wrong with keeping a lost item that you happen to find?
2. Why did Lynette wait to turn in the bracelet?
3. Why was she afraid to turn it in later?
4. Why did Anna feel that turning in the bracelet was her responsibility, too?
5. Was Lynette being responsible when she kept the bracelet and didn't contact Mrs. Smith about returning it to its owner? In the end was she demonstrating responsibility when she returned it? Explain your answer.
6. What does it mean to be a responsible person?
7. What does it mean to take responsibility for your actions?

Anna and the Silver Bracelet
Reflection Sheet

Think about the story of Anna, whose friend found a bracelet and almost kept it. Write your answers to these questions:

1. Have you ever lost something and gotten it back because the person who found it was responsible and honest? Describe what happened:

2. Have you ever found something and turned it in? Why did you turn in the item, and how did you feel about your actions?

3. You've probably heard the saying, "Finders keepers, losers weepers." Maybe you've even said it yourself. What's wrong with the ideas behind that saying?

Framing the Blame Game
Cartooning and Discussion

This activity teaches children to:

— describe situations involving denial of responsibility or blaming.
— explain the importance and benefits of accepting responsibility for their actions.
— creatively demonstrate the contrast between blaming and being responsible in specific situations.

You will need:

drawing paper; colored markers, pencils, or crayons; sample cartoon strips clipped from the newspaper or taken off the internet

Directions:

Begin by asking your child/children how they feel when they get blamed for something they didn't do. Listen to their responses, and then ask: *Have you ever been in a situation where a person has done something wrong or made a mistake, and you know it, but the person denies it?*

Point out that when we deny responsibility for our actions, we are in effect blaming someone else — even if we don't actually point a finger at someone and say "she did it."

Give your child/children several examples of blaming and elicit many more from them. Here are some possibilities:

- A child with frosting on their face denies having eaten a piece of cake.
- A child fails a test and says the teacher is stupid or unfair.
- A man has a car accident and blames his wife because she was talking and taking his attention away from the road.
- A person is late for work and blames the heavy traffic.
- A teenager breaks his mother's favorite vase and says that it shouldn't

have been so close to the edge of the shelf.
- A batter keeps missing the ball and claims the pitcher is lousy, the sun is in his eyes, and the spectators are making him nervous.
- A child is caught shoplifting and tells her mother, "The other kids made me do it."

Announce that they are going to make pairs of cartoon strips, one showing a blaming situation, and the other showing the same situation but with the "guilty" character accepting responsibility in the last frame. Show and read aloud the sample cartoon strips to your child/children. Explain that these cartoons are models they can use to see how a cartoon is depicted in a very simple way in each frame.

Distribute the art materials. Suggest that your child/children illustrate a situation from their own experience, or one that was mentioned in the earlier discussion. Remind your child/children not to use real names. Stipulate that each cartoon strip should have at least three frames, showing:

1. the incident (mistake or wrongdoing)
2. the decision concerning what to do (showing fear, guilt, confusion, inner struggle, etc.)
3. blaming/denying or acceptance of responsibility

Anyone whose situations require additional frames should be urged to limit the number to a maximum of six.

When the cartoons are finished, end the activity by facilitating a discussion.

Questions for Discussion and Reflection:

1. Why is it hard to admit when you are wrong?
2. When you make a mess, whose job is it to clean it up? Why?
3. Does anyone ever really make you do something? Explain.
4. How do we benefit by admitting our mistakes and taking responsibility?
5. What are some of the things that can happen if we don't accept responsibility?
6. What have you learned from this activity?

Variation:

Instead of making cartoons (or as an alternative for some children), allow teams to develop two skits, one dramatizing a blaming situation and the other showing the same situation with the character accepting responsibility.

Note:

An excellent internet resource for using comics with your child/children is *www.makebeliefscomix.com*.

Responsibility In Action
Self-Assessment and Discussion

This activity teaches children to:
— identify specific examples of responsible behavior.
— monitor and describe in writing responsible and irresponsible behaviors for a prescribed period.

What you will need:
two or more copies of the Responsibility Log for each child; chart paper

Directions:

Begin by discussing the meaning of the word *responsibility*. List the following four components of responsibility on the chart paper. Discuss the nonspecific examples that are listed under each of the four components. Ask your child/children to think of specific examples that might fit under each of the four components. These can be incidents from their own lives or something they have observed others doing. Share your own specific examples, too.

Accountability
- Think before you act.
- Before you make a decision or take an action, think about how it will affect the other people involved. What will be the consequences?
- When you do something wrong or make a mistake, admit it and accept the consequences. Don't blame others or make excuses.
- Give credit to others for their achievements.
- Do what you should do, or have agreed to do, even if it is difficult.

Excellence
- Set a good example in everything you do.
- Do your best.
- Keep trying — don't quit.
- Make it your goal to always be proud of your performance (schoolwork, homework, projects, completed chores, athletic, or other performances, etc.)

Self-control or self-restraint
- Always control yourself.
- Control your temper — don't throw things, scream, hit others, or use bad language.
- Wait your turn.
- Show courtesy and good manners.

Being a good sport
- Win and lose with grace
- Accept congratulations when you win; accept responsibility when you lose.
- Take pride in how you play the game, not just whether you win.

Continue the discussion until your child/children understand the meaning of responsibility and many specific examples of responsible behavior have been shared. Then announce that, for the next few days, they are going to keep logs describing actions that are clearly responsible and clearly not responsible.

Distribute the "Responsibility Log" and go over the directions. Explain that they should write down actions that they know are responsible (doing their best on an assignment and completing it on time; admitting when they forget to do a chore; congratulating the other team when they lose a game, etc.) as well as actions they feel *are not* responsible (not paying attention when someone is talking to them, blaming another person, procrastinating on an assignment, etc.).

Announce a date when the completed logs are due. Allow from two to five days, depending on the maturity of your child/children. Commend (for their responsibility) those who complete the logs on time.

Before collecting the logs, have your child/children share their results. Finally, lead a culminating discussion.

Questions for Discussion and Reflection:

1. Which do you have more of on your logs, actions which are responsible or actions which are not responsible?
2. What surprised you about the results of your log?
3. How do you feel when you take a responsible action? How do you feel when your actions are not responsible?
4. In which area of responsibility do you think you need to improve?

Responsibility Log

For the next few days, pay close attention to your actions. Write down things you say and do that are clearly responsible actions. Also, write down things you say and do that you realize are not responsible actions.

Action	Responsible? Yes or No	Reactions of Others	I Learned

A Time I Helped Without Being Asked
A Sharing Circle

This Sharing Circle teaches children to:

— describe the difference between choosing to do something and being told to do it.
— state the importance of assuming responsibility for things that need to be done.

Introduce the Topic:

Today we're going to talk about taking the initiative — about accepting responsibility without being told to by an adult. Our topic is, "A Time I Helped Without Being Asked."

Think of a time when something that needed to be done and took it upon yourself to do it. No one had to tell you or ask you or even hint to you that it needed doing. Maybe you walked into the kitchen and saw a sink full of dirty dishes and, instead of just ignoring it, you cleaned it up. Or maybe you saw someone break something and you helped pick up the pieces. Perhaps a neighbor was searching for a missing pet and you joined in. Or you might have stayed to help a friend clean up their yard after playing games there. You can probably think of lots of times when you decided on your own to take responsibility. Tell us about one of those times. The topic is, "A Time I Helped Without Being Asked."

Questions for Discussion and Reelection:

1. How did you feel when you helped without being asked?
2. How would your feelings have been different if you had been asked, or even ordered, to do the same thing?
3. What does it mean to be a responsible person?
4. Why is it important for each of us to take responsibility for things that need to be done?

A Time I Behaved Responsibly

A Sharing Circle

This Sharing Circle teaches children to:

—define responsible behavior.
—describe a situation in which they behaved responsibly.
—discuss the benefits of responsible behavior.

Introduce the Topic:

Say to your child/children: *Today, let's take some deserved credit and talk about "A Time I Behaved Responsibly." Before we go any further, let's take a couple of minutes to discuss what responsible behavior is and why people think it's so important. Do you have any ideas?*

Listen to everyone's comments. Then, in your own words, explain: *The word itself, response-able, says a lot. It means being able to respond, to do something you think is right, not just sit there and do nothing. In other words, when you take care of a situation and yourself, you've behaved responsibly. You can feel proud of yourself. It may have been simple, or it may have been hard, but you did it! Think that over. You can probably remember lots of times when you behaved responsibly. See if there isn't one you'd like to tell us about. If there is, we'd like to hear what happened, how you felt, and what you did. The topic is, "A Time I Behaved Responsibly".*

Questions for Discussion and Reflection:

1. How do you feel now about the responsible behavior you described?
2. What rewards do you get for responsible behavior?
3. What are some of the consequences of irresponsible behavior?
4. Did you hear any good ideas for ways to behave responsibly that you might not have thought of before?

What Did You Learn About Responsibility?

Use this page to think about and record the things you have learned about responsibility. You can write, draw pictures, scribble and doodle, create a poem, or anything else that has meaning to you and will help you remember what you have learned.

When you finish, show this page to someone else and explain what you have learned.

SELF-CONTROL

"Self Control is the power within you that holds the reins of anger, intolerance, and impulsiveness."

Remez Sasson

Tips for Teaching Self-Control:

You are your child's most important teacher! Model the kind of behavior you hope to see your child display. If you are trying to teach self-control, but lash out angrily when your child misbehaves, they will learn to do as you do, not as you say.

Help your child to think about the consequences of his or her behavior. Remember to praise your child for doing things that demonstrate self-control.

Talk with your child about self-control. When you're watching television or in real life and you notice a person acting badly, comment to your child about what that person is doing, and how that behavior reflects a lack of self-control. Discuss what you see, and hear. Ask questions such as, "What could that person have done differently instead of...?"

Vocabulary Words

- Approximately
- Irritable
- Claim
- Scuffling
- Chatter
- Collision
- Careened
- Angular
- Pivoting
- Briskly
- Drawl
- Contraption
- Struggle
- Blare
- Employment

An Alterna-Tive Tale

The Want family lived in a big, sturdy house with a yard the size of a small park on a quiet street in the town of Amity.

It was a good thing that the house was big, because fully sixteen Wants ranging in age from eighteen months to 73 years lived within its walls. It was an even better thing that the walls were thick and sturdy, because the Wants tended to be — well, *loud* probably says it best. And it was indeed fortunate that the yard was deep enough to keep the house well back from the quiet street — or it would not have been quiet at all.

The reason for all the noise in the Want house can be summed up in one word — *confusion*. It wasn't that the Wants didn't love one another — they did. But they were active, independent people and it seemed as though every Want always wanted something different from every other Want.

For example, at around seven o'clock each weekday morning, approximately thirteen hungry, hurrying Wants would arrive in the kitchen eager for breakfast. These were the family members who needed to leave for work or school. They were always rushed and often irritable. If four of them wanted eggs, you could be sure that only one preferred scrambled, while the other three insisted on fried, poached, and boiled. Assuming they were lucky enough to find four pans and fit them on the four burners of the stove, this left no room for the Wants who hurried in wanting to fix oatmeal, french toast, pancakes, or to boil water for tea.

At nine o'clock at night, cries went up for more than a dozen different TV shows. And on Saturday morning, at least nine or ten Wants would claim to need one of the family's two cars for errands or activities that had absolutely no relation in time or location to one another.

The only time two Wants ever wanted the same thing was when there was only one of it. For instance, Wilbur and Winnifred could always be counted on to want the washing machine at the same hour of the same day. And if there was only one light bulb left, at least five desktop or bedside reading lamps would blow out at virtually the same instant. You can probably imagine how it was in the Want house. Arguments, yelling, endless discussions, and very few decisions. Rarely could people agree on who should go to the store and buy the groceries. Or what groceries ought to be bought. Or how they ought to be prepared. There were always sixteen different ideas about where the Christmas tree should be placed, and eleven volunteers who wanted to put the angel on the top of the tree.

Visiting home from college one weekend, Wanda Want (who was studying business management) said, "What this family needs most is a household manager. Maybe then some decisions would get made."

This suggestion was followed by a loud and lively discussion among several members of the family. Everyone had a slightly different viewpoint, and everyone expressed it. Of course, no agreements were reached so no decisions were made. Wiley and Wilomena went off to the kitchen table and tried to write a want ad — together. They argued about it for hours. They couldn't agree on what a household manager should do. They couldn't even decide how many lines to write, or where to place the ad, or when to stop arguing and eat lunch.

Finally, Wanda wrote the ad herself. She was smart enough not to ask for anyone else's ideas or reactions. But when it appeared in the newspaper, she cut it out and posted it on the front of the refrigerator for everyone to see:

Full-time Household Manager wanted for very large, active family. Cooking and cleaning not required. Must know how to promote self-control, conflict resolution, and decision making. Call 756-8742 weekdays after 7:00 p.m. and ask for Wanda.

The phone number was for Wanda's college dormitory. For the next two weeks, Wanda conducted interviews during the week. When she came home on the first Friday night, she refused to discuss the progress of her plan with any member of the family. But when she came home at the end of the second week, Wanda made an announcement. She said, "Tomorrow morning at 10:00 a.m., the Want Family Household Manager will arrive for her first day of work. I would like all of you to be present." Then, without another word, she climbed the stairs to her room.

On Saturday morning at exactly 10:00 a.m., the doorbell rang. For one glorious moment, every activity, every discussion, and every argument stopped. The Want house was silent.

Then it exploded. Dishes and pans clattered into the sink, chair legs scraped across the floor and doors in every corner of the house swung open and slammed shut. The sound of running, walking and scuffling footsteps mixed with whispered chatter, yelling and laughter as everyone hurried to the door.

A collision was inevitable. Weld and Wendy slid into the entryway and dove for the door as if it were first base at a Little League game. William dove for the door from halfway up the entry staircase, and Winter careened down the hall on her skateboard. There was a loud crash. The front door shuddered and rattled on its hinges — then burst open to reveal four young Wants in a heap on the floor surrounded by a curious (and curious-looking) crowd of twelve onlookers.

Leaning against the porch railing was a tall, angular woman with black hair and knowing dark eyes. Her arms were folded loosely across the front of a bright yellow warm-up suit. A smile of amusement played at one corner of her broad mouth. Leaning on its end against the railing next to the women was a long leather carrying case that almost equaled her in height.

The woman watched with interest as Weld, Wendy, William and Winter untangled themselves. Then she picked up her carrying case and stepped through the door without being asked. Breaking a path across the entryway, the woman walked briskly to the living room and stopped.

"My name is Alterna," she said, pivoting smoothly to survey her audience. "Alterna Tive." Alterna looked steadily into sixteen pairs of eyes — one pair at a time. A grin traveled back and forth between her large ears. "Rhymes with jive," she added in an exaggerated drawl.

Everyone stared, speechless. Then Wanda stepped forward. "Welcome Alterna," she said, extending her hand. "Allow me to introduce my family." Wanda moved down the line and Alterna followed her, shaking hands and repeating each person's name. "Weston, Wisteria, Wooley, Walter…"

When the introductions were over, Alterna stepped back and asked cheerfully, "Well, what's everybody doing today?"

"Shopping!"

"Homework!"

"Little League!"

"The lake!"

"Weston can't go fishing 'til he mows the lawn," said Winter, loudly.

"It's not my turn," yelled Weston. "It's yours, and you know it!"

"I did it last week."

"Well, somebody else will have to do it then, because I get stuck with that job all the time," Weston said firmly.

Alterna was unzipping her carrying case. She reached in and lifted out a leggy metal contraption and, with a few pulls and snaps, transformed it into an easel. Then she unrolled a pad of paper and hung it from the top of the easel. A fat, black pen appeared in her hand.

"It's a big yard," observed Alterna, holding up her hand to quiet the group. "I bet that when you do the yard work, it takes you all day."

Nodding heads — and groans.

"If you've done yard work even once during the last year, come up here and sign your name," said Alterna, tossing her pen to Weston.

Two minutes later, the chart had nine names on it.

"Hey, look at what you just did," exclaimed Alterna. "There was only one pen and you took turns using it. And I didn't even have to tell you to!"

Shrugs and giggles.

Alterna studied the list. "So, this is the yard team," she said. "Is there anyone else who would like to be on the yard team?"

Seven-year-old Woody stepped forward. "Me," he announced. Alterna gave him the pen and he signed his name.

"Let's see," said Alterna, "we have one big yard, and one big team with ten individual members. How many ways can a team of ten make sure that the yard gets cleaned every week?"

"Take turns."

"Make a schedule."

"Do it together."

"Divide up the work."

"Divide up the yard."

"Have two teams of five, and appoint judges to decide which team did the best work."

"Or the fastest!"

"And award a prize!"

Alterna was writing all the ideas down on a clean sheet of paper. "Tell you what," she smiled. "I think the team has some terrific ideas. And I think the team can find a solution to the problem without the rest of us hanging around. Weston, since you seem to have the most yard experience, you're in charge of this meeting. Here's the pen — and here are the rules."

Alterna looked from one team member to another. "Only one person talks at a time. Everybody else listens. Keep listing ideas until you run out of them. Then use the ideas to create a solution. The solution doesn't have to be perfect, but it has to be one that every member of the team will agree to try for at least two weeks. No exceptions. Okay? We'll check back with you later."

Alterna went with the rest of the family into the kitchen. "I could sure use a cup of tea," she said. "Do you have any?"

"I'll fix it," offered Wayne.

"No, let me do it," begged Wilomena.

They began to struggle over the tea kettle.

"Hold it!" cried Alterna. "Let me have the kettle for a second."

Alterna shook the tea kettle to make certain it was empty and then placed it on the floor and gave it a spin. "When it stops, the person closest to where the spout is pointing gets to make the tea. And since I drink a lot of tea, the other person gets to make it next time."

Wayne won the spin. He fixed spicy orange tea for everyone.

Throughout the day, Alterna Tive migrated from one part of the house to another, watching the Wants closely, and jumping in whenever an argument erupted, which of course was often. When a conflict was complicated, Alterna used her easel. Most of the time, she just used her head.

"Where do you think you're going with those car keys," demanded Wilbur. He was chasing Wysteria down the hall.

"I have to pick up Wendy and Weld from Little League practice," called Wysteria over her shoulder. She quickened her pace.

"You don't have to leave yet. The practice isn't over for another hour," shouted Wilbur. "I was just about to run over to the building-supply store."

"There's a sale on sheets at the department store. I have to stop there first."

Wysteria was out the door, with Wilbur in hot pursuit. "I won't be able to fix the screen door today," insisted Wilbur.

"Wilbur, I have to go now because this is the last day of the sale. Why can't you just wait till I get back."

"Because it will be too late," shouted Wilbur in reply. "I have to fix the screen before dark."

Wysteria lifted the garage door. "No you don't. It's been broken for a month. Another day won't hurt."

"I don't want to wait another day! I want to do it today!"

The battle was broken by the blare of the car horn. When she had captured their attention, Alterna pulled her arm from the driver's window of the car and stepped out of the garage. "My goodness," she scolded. "Two smart people putting all their energy into fighting over one car. Why don't you put your energy into finding a way to share the car and accomplish all three errands — the sheets, the building supplies, and the Little League pick up."

Wilbur stared at the ground and grumbled. Wysteria looked embarrassed. "Maybe you could pick up the kids," she said. "After you get your supplies." Wysteria offered Wilbur the car keys.

"Yeah, I could do that, but then you'd miss the sheet sale."

"No," said Wysteria. "I could go after you get back."

"Or I could drop you off at the department store first, and pick you up after I pick up Weld and Wendy," suggested Wilbur.

"That might be better," said Wysteria. "Come on. Let's not waste any more time."

Alterna stayed for dinner. Between the pasta and the pie, she made an announcement. "Before I leave tonight," she said. "I am going to appoint two people to be systems managers for the next week. My experience has taught me that a lot of conflicts can be avoided if you take the time to set things up right from the beginning. For example, a systems manager might design a car-use schedule and post it near the door. People who wanted to use one of the cars would sign for it in advance. Another thing a systems manager might do is notice when the family is running out of something that everybody uses — like shampoo or bananas — and put that item on the shopping list. As a systems manager, your job is to pay attention to the kinds of conflicts people have, and then try to figure out ways of preventing them."

All but two Wants immediately applied for the position of systems manager. "I have fourteen applicants for two jobs," said Alterna. She paused for several seconds and then asked matter-of-factly, "Who would be willing to withdraw his or her application and wait till another week?"

Three Wants withdrew.

"That leaves eleven applicants for two jobs," said Alterna patiently. "You know, if they want to, systems managers can ask for advice and suggestions. Maybe some of you would be willing to serve as advisors this week — if you're asked to that is."

Seven more Wants withdrew their applications.

"That leaves four applicants for two jobs," said Alterna. "I need two more withdrawals."

"Wait a minute," chimed in Walter. "Who says that a job has to be for just one person? Why can't each job be filled by a team of two?"

A chorus of approval sounded from around the dining table. Alterna grinned and gestured her thumbs-up approval. "Now you're really getting the idea!" she laughed.

"Alterna," asked little Wooley. "Are you coming back every Saturday?"

"I think two or three more Saturdays will be enough," replied Alterna. "After that, you won't need me anymore. In my business," smiled Alterna broadly, "short-term employment is a sign of success."

Questions for Discussion and Reflection:

1. What are some examples of self-control that you heard in this story? When did the characters show a lack of self-control?
2. Why is it important for only one person to talk at a time when you are trying to solve a problem?
3. Why did Alterna tell the yard team that its solution for doing yard work didn't have to be perfect?
4. Spinning the kettle on the floor was a game of chance. What are some other games of chance that can be used to settle conflicts?
5. How can we keep from getting locked into seeing just one solution — our own?
6. Why do you think Wysteria was embarrassed when Alterna found her and Wilbur fighting over the car?
7. What did Alterna do to help the 14 applicants avoid a conflict over the systems manager job?

An Alterna-Tive Tale
Reflection Sheet

What did you learn about self-control from the story of the Want family? What did you learn about solving conflicts? Think about the story as you answer these questions:

1. Write about a time when you had to really demonstrate self-control. What happened, and what did you do?

2. Think of a conflict you have had with someone. Are there ways that conflict could have been prevented? If so, how? If not, why?

3. Alterna Tive got her name from the word alternative. It's a perfect name for her. Can you explain why?

A Wave of Self-Control
Brainstorm, Sharing, and Discussion

This activity teaches children to:

— spontaneously complete sentences related to self-control.
— identify do's and don'ts related to self-control.
— describe how having specific behavioral goals can lead to greater self-control.

You will need:

chart paper, writing paper, paper bags

Directions:

Write the sentence starters listed below on separate pieces of paper. Fold them up and put them into a paper bag. Have your child/children pull a sentence starter out of the bag and state an ending. Depending on the number of children you are working with, you may want to do two or three rounds so that each child responds to several sentence starters and all sentence starters are responded to. If working with one child, you can limit the number of sentences, or you and your child can take turns responding

Sentence Starters

- When I'm angry at someone, I usually...
- A good way to control my temper is to...
- A rule I have trouble following is...
- Self-control is important because...
- I sometimes get in trouble for...
- I get impatient about...
- I don't like waiting for...
- I'm getting better about controlling...
- When I feel impatient, I...
- A good way to blow off steam is...

Next, point out that all of the sentence starters had to do with self-control. (Or ask your child/children to guess the central theme.)

Explain that having self-control is part of being a responsible person. If you have self-control, you are able to *manage* and *regulate* your own behavior. Ask your child/children to name some *do's* and *don'ts* associated with self-control. Write their suggestions on the chart paper, creating a "Do" list and a "Don't" list that contain items like these:

DO:

raise your hand
wait your turn
sit quietly
be polite
have consideration
be patient
show respect for others
be understanding

DON'T:

fidget
interrupt
lose your temper
throw things
scream
hit others
use bad language.

Ask your child/children how they might go about gaining more self-control. Listen to their suggestions, and write these steps on the chart paper:

1. Decide exactly what behavior you want to change.
2. Set a self-control goal.
3. Think of things you can do, or not do, to help yourself reach your goal.
4. Keep working on the new behavior, little by little, until it becomes a habit.

Discuss these steps with your child/children.

Give them a personal example or use this one:

Rick had a hard time keeping his room clean. He set a goal to develop the habit of picking up his things every morning before school and every evening at bedtime. Since he shared the room with his younger brother, Mike, Rick had to enlist Mike's cooperation. He decided to organize the closet and the shelves so that his books, toys, and other gear were kept separate from Mike's. When Mike left things lying around, Rick would ask nicely, "Please pick that up — I'm working on my goal." Each day he spent a little time doing the tasks that needed to be done, and eventually his parents no longer had to scold him about keeping his room clean. He had achieved his goal!

Conclude the activity with further discussion.

Questions for Discussion and Reflection:

1. How much self-control do babies have?
2. Do you think people gain more self-control as they grow up? Why or why not?
3. Is gaining self-control as you get older automatic, or do you have to work at it? Explain.
4. Over what behavior would you like to have more control?

Extension:

Use this activity as a springboard to helping your child/children set self-control goals. Work through this goal-setting process with your child/children on a one-to-one basis. Draw and duplicate a picture of a target on a sheet of paper. Within the target make a number of concentric circles. Have your child/children identify and write their self-control goal in the center, bulls eye, of the target. Every day that a child shows progress toward his or her individual self-control goal (which should be written on the sheet), allow the child to color in one of the circles, starting with the outside edge of the target and working toward the center. Use many different colors. When the entire target is filled in, congratulate the child for reaching his or her goal.

Learning to Control My Anger

Discussion and Reflection Sheet

This activity teaches children to:

— describe examples of self-control and self-management.
— demonstrate behaviors associated with self-control.
— affirm themselves for their own levels of self-control.

You will need:

one copy of the reflection sheet, "I Can Control My Anger," for each child

Directions:

Lead your child/children in a discussion about anger. Acknowledge that it is an uncomfortable emotion that can sometimes be difficult to control. However, emphasizing that it is normal to feel angry at times. Make these additional points:

- Anger is a normal human emotion. It is neither bad nor good in itself.
- Volatile expressions of anger, if they happen often, can negatively affect relationships and can have negative health consequences as well.
- There are healthy and appropriate ways to manage anger.
- It is how we react to a situation, not the situation itself, that causes anger and other emotions.

Ask your child/children to share the feelings they get inside when they are angry. Next, ask them to think of ways they can appropriately express this energy that builds up inside as a result of anger. Have them come up with healthy and acceptable ways of dealing with anger. Write all their suggestions on the chart paper and discuss.

Discuss the idea that if people know what makes them angry, they can learn to recognize the onset of angry feelings and can do something to calm down or cool down.

Distribute the reflection sheets and go over the directions (or have your child/children make their own reflection sheet by folding a sheet of paper in half the long way and writing the headings at the top of each fold). Give your child/children time to list situations and conditions that make them angry and ways to manage the anger. When they have finished, have them read the items they have listed in each column.

Elaborate on each example and use it to generate further discussion. Focus less on the situations (and their justification) and more on anger-management strategies. Encourage your child/children to keep their sheets in a place where they can refer to them often.

Questions for Discussion and Reflection:

1. Why is it important to control anger?
2. What are the most common causes of anger that we identified?
3. What ideas for controlling anger work best for you?
4. What can you do if nothing you try helps to lessen your anger?
5. What happens when people are unable to control their anger?
6. What new ideas for controlling anger would you like to try?
7. What happens if you let anger build up inside over hours or days?

Extend the Learning

Teach your child/children to remember the acronym STOP whenever they feel their anger or stress level rising.

S=Stop what your doing.

T=Take several deep breaths.

O=Observe, without judging, what you're feeling and thinking.

P=Proceed with your day in a calm and in-control manner.

Point out that this simple exercise will help them calm down in the moment but also helps to retrain their automatic response to anger and stress, so they stay calmer and more in control in future situations.

I Can Control My Anger
Reflection Sheet

Do certain things almost always make you angry? Do you react angrily to the same situations-or the same people-over and over? Maybe you get angry when you don't get your way. Or when your brother or sister uses your things without asking.

In the left column, list things that usually make you angry. In the right column, list things you can do to deal with your angry feelings.

What Makes Me Angry	**What I Can Do to Control My Anger**
1.	
2.	
3.	
4.	
5.	
6.	
7.	
8.	
9.	
10.	

A Time I Felt Anger and Handled It Well

A Sharing Circle

This Sharing Circle teaches children to:

— verbally acknowledge themselves and others for successfully controlling anger.
— identify techniques for controlling anger.

Introduce the Topic:

Anger is one of the hardest emotions to deal with. It doesn't feel good and it's hard to control. In this session, we're going to talk about successfully controlling anger. Our topic is, "A Time I Felt Anger and Handled It Well."

Think of a time when you were angry at something or someone, but you bit your lip, or counted to ten, or did something else to keep from blowing up. You may have been mad at a friend, parent, teacher, brother or sister, and it could have been over something important or a tiny thing. Tell us what happened and what you did to control yourself, but please don't mention any names. The topic is, "A Time I Felt Anger and Handled It Well."

Questions for Discussion and Reflection:

1. Why is it important to control anger? What kinds of things can anger lead to if it isn't controlled?
2. What are some ways to let anger out, like air from a balloon, without actually getting angry?
3. What have you learned about anger and self-control from this session?

A Time I Accepted Someone Else's Anger
A Sharing Circle

This Sharing Circle teaches children to:

— describe ways of diffusing another person's anger.
— explain that to manage anger requires self-control.

Introduce the Topic:

Anger is a difficult emotion to handle when you feel it inside, and also when someone else's anger is coming directly at you. It's hard to just stand there and catch anger the way you do a softball. But we've all done it, and that's what were going to talk about today. Our topic is, "A Time I Accepted Someone Else's Anger."

Think about a time when someone was angry at you, and instead of being angry back, or getting defensive, you just accepted the anger. Like a baseball catcher, you let the anger come right at you and caught it, and because you were prepared to catch the anger, it didn't hurt so much. Maybe a parent was angry at you for something, and you accepted the anger. Or perhaps a friend was angry at you, but you knew it was mostly because your friend was in a bad mood, so you were patient and let it happen. Tell us the circumstances without mentioning any names, and describe how you stayed in control. The topic is, "A Time I Accepted Someone Else's Anger."

Questions for Discussion and Reflection:

1. Why is another person's anger so difficult to accept?
2. What is the first thing you want to do when someone is angry at you?
3. Why do you think it helps to just accept the other person's anger and not do anything back?
4. What have you learned about anger from this session? ...about self-control?

What Did You Learn About Self-Control?

Use this page to think about and record the things you have learned about self-control. You can write, draw pictures, scribble and doodle, create a poem, or anything else that has meaning to you and will help you remember what you have learned.

When you finish, show this page to someone else and explain what you have learned.

MAKING GOOD DECISIONS

"Our deeds still travel with us from afar, and what we have been makes us what we are."

George Eliot

Tips for Teaching Kids How to Make Good Decisions:

When you give your child opportunities to make their own choices, you are teaching problem solving and independence. Giving your child ways to express preferences and make decisions shows that their ideas and feelings matter. Your child's self-confidence deepens and leads to better decision making and less likelihood of being swayed by negative influences.

Teach by example. Children take note of what is going on around them. They are learning from what they observe others doing. When appropriate, share with children decisions you are making and how you arrived at the final decision. Tell them about how you have evaluated different outcomes and how you considered the consequences, and effects of your choices on others.

Vocabulary Words

- Gurgled
- Wobbled/wobbliness
- Cowardice
- Juvenile Delinquent
- Wrath
- Annoyed
- Murmured
- Goad
- Dominated
- Harmlessly

Sweet Revenge

"Dare you!" Morey said.

I gulped. Morey had dared me before to do things I didn't want to do, like ten pull-ups on the high bar, or kick the girl's ball when they were playing a game. Once he even dared me to stick out my tongue at the store clerk while she wasn't looking, which I did, though I could have sworn she saw me at the last minute when she turned her head and I yanked my tongue quickly into hiding.

Truth is, I was weary of Morey's dares, and today's felt worse than ever before. My stomach gurgled like an empty cavern. My legs felt rubbery — I wobbled like a Saturday morning cartoon character.

I was standing with Morey and three other boys right below Mr. Brickle's big picture window, where Mr. Brickle stood every day and watched us kids walk home. If he saw anyone goofing off, or bothering the girls, or — worst of all — stepping on his property in the slightest, on any part, the grass or the flower bed with tulip bulbs waiting for Spring, he'd pound on the window and shake his fist at us. And if that didn't work, he'd disappear from view for a moment, then reappear on the porch shouting, "You kids better stay out of my yard if you know what's good for you!" None of us ever really knew what wouldn't be good for us if we didn't stay out of his yard, but we never had the courage to defy the old man and find out. Until now that is.

All eyes were on me, the growing silence giving away my cowardice in the face of pressure. I didn't know which was worse, the fear of Brickle or the fear of saying no to my friends.

"Come on, James," one of the guys urged. "Are you or aren't you?"

"Yeah. You're the one who's always talking so tough, saying 'Mr. Brickle is as dumb as a pickle,' and stuff like that. Are you going to throw that rock or not?"

I admit, I'd wanted to get even for a long time — ever since Brickle yelled at me for parking my bike on the sidewalk in front of his house while I ran after my dog. When I came back the bike was gone, and I didn't get it back for a week. My parents made me go over and apologize to Mr. Brickle, even though they agreed that I hadn't done anything wrong. The sidewalk was public property. Only problem was, Mr. Brickle or someone else walking by might have fallen trying to go around the bike blocking their way.

That same night after dinner, my buddies and I had met on the corner of Mr. Brickle's street and talked about getting even with the old man by breaking his precious picture window. Then he couldn't stand there and stare at us anymore. Morey was convinced that tonight was the perfect time, since we'd seen Mr. Brickle's son drive off with him. It was twilight, dark enough so we couldn't be seen from the street in the bushes beneath the window, but light enough for Morey to find the medium-sized rock he now held out to me.

"You're chicken, James," one of the guys said. "All talk and no action," said another.

"Well, you do it then, Big Mouth," I shot back.

"He didn't take my bike, man."

"Yeah, but he's yelled at you as much as me, calling you a punk kid and a juvenile delinquent."

The other boys murmured agreement. It was true. Brickle had insulted us all at one time or another. Not one kid who walked by his house had been spared the wrath of his cruel words. Hadn't Mr. Brickle ever been a kid? What was wrong with him anyway?

"Well, James?" they all echoed in unison. "It's getting dark. Let's go. Now or never."

"Okay, okay." I was starting to feel annoyed at the pressure. I figured they were just as scared as I was, that's why they were trying to goad me into doing it. Breaking someone's window was wrong — even the window of a mean old man like Brickle.

I decided to fake them out. "I'll do it on one condition," I said.

"What?" asked Morey.

"That we're all in this together. If anyone gets caught, we all get caught. And if anyone runs, the deal is off. Got it?"

They all looked at each other for a moment, then back at me.

"Okay. Do it."

I stepped back so I could see the front of the house, dominated by the window. It was an old wooden house, built over eighty years ago, with brick around the bottom. The section with the big window jutted out toward the street, so while it provided a perfect viewing stand for Mr. Brickle, it also made a perfect target.

I tossed the rock up and down in my palm, higher each time. I eyed the glass as though it were a bull's-eye on a shooting range. "Let's get Brickle, let's get Brickle," I began to chant. My arm was up in the air now, making circles as if I was preparing to throw the rock all the way to China. "Get Brickle, get Brickle, get Brickle."

"Quiet!" hissed Morey. "You want everyone in the neighborhood to hear you?"

Ignoring Morey's warning, I shouted, "Spread out guys, so you don't get hit by flying glass! Here I go... one, two..."

"RUN!" cried Morey as they all scattered like squirrels fleeing the hunter.

"Three!"

I held onto the rock for a moment before letting it drop harmlessly to the ground. I turned away just in time to see the other guys disappear around a corner.

Heading home, I noticed that the wobbliness in my legs was gone. I started to whistle a tune. "What'll Morey come up with next?" I wondered.

Questions for Discussion and Reflection::

1. Did Mr. Brickle show respect for children who walked by his house? ?
2. Did children show respect for Mr. Brickle? How did they feel about him?
3. Did the fact that Mr. Brickle was a mean person make it all right to destroy his property? Why?
4. Was it right or wrong of Mr. Brickle to take James' bike?
5. How would you have felt if you were James? What would you have done?
6. How else could the boys have handled their anger at Mr. Brickle?
7. Did James really want to break the window? How do you know?
8. What are some other ways that James could have resisted the pressure of his friends?
9. How do you think James felt as he headed home?
10. In the end did James make a good decision not to throw the rock through Mr. Brickle's window? Explain.

Sweet Revenge

Reflection Sheet

Think about the story of James and his friends and how James made a good decision in the way he handled the pressure the other boys put on him to do something he knew was wrong.

1. What would you have said and done if you were James?

2. Have you ever been pressured by other kids to do something wrong? What kinds of things did they say and do to pressure you?

3. How did you react to the pressure? Did you go along with them or did you resist in some way?

4. Think about a time you made a good decision and write about how you felt

Dozens of Ways to Say No
Brainstorming, Role Play and Discussion

This activity teaches children to:

— distinguish between friendly and teasing forms of peer pressure.
— formulate and practice specific ways of saying no to peer pressure.

You will need:

chart paper; markers or pens and paper for children to write on

Directions:

Provide a sheet of paper and have pens and markers available.

Write the word, *friendly* on the chart paper and draw a smiley face next to it. Remind your child/children that sometimes peer pressure comes in friendly forms — from kids they know and like. Perhaps the hardest thing about saying no to friendly pressure is the fear of hurting a relationship or losing a friend. But by saying no in a friendly way, they can stand up for themselves while at the same time reassuring their friend that they like and value him or her. They may even influence their friend to say no, too. Offer some examples of friendly responses (see end of activity).

Tell your child/children to come up with as many friendly ways of saying "no" as they can think of in five minutes and to write each down on their paper

Next, write the word *teasing* on the chart paper and draw a smirky face next to it. Remind your child/children that dares, bribes, put downs and other forms of teasing are also used to pressure us to do things we shouldn't do. One of the hardest things about saying "no" to teasing pressure is not wanting to look foolish, dumb, or weak. Learning "snappy" ways to say no can help. Offer some examples of snappy responses (see end of activity).

Ask your child/children to write down as many snappy ways of saying no as they can think of in 5 minutes. Encourage them to collaborate and to have fun.

Have your child/children read their friendly and snappy responses. Write these on the chart paper as they are shared under the appropriate column. Display the lists where they can be referred to.

Practice using the responses. Have your child/children role play peer pressure situations, such as offering them alcohol and other drugs, or goading them into unethical or illegal acts. Vary your invitations from friendly to teasing. Have your child/children pick their responses from the posted lists. Encourage them to stand, and to use appropriate posture, gestures, facial expressions, volume, etc.

Conclude the activity with a general discussion.

Questions for Discussion and Reflection:

1. Why is it sometimes hard to say no to a friend?
2. If a friend gets mad at you when you say no, what can you do to feel better about it?
3. Why does it help to practice saying no in different ways?
4. When you are being pressured to do something you know is wrong, how can being prepared with some friendly and snappy ways to say no help you to make the best decision on what to do?

Note: Role play is a powerful experiential activity that helps children to be prepared with healthy responses and behaviors when confronted with real life challenges. You can use role play often as a teaching tool.

Sample Friendly Responses

— No, I really don't want to.
— I'd like to go to your party, but if no adults are going to be there I can't.
— No thanks. Why don't we ride bikes instead?
— I don't want to mess up my mind, and I wish you wouldn't mess up yours either.
— No, I never put this body in dangerous situations. Let's think of something else to do.

Sample Snappy Responses

— No thanks, I'd rather walk my pet python.
— I'm not interested. I've got better things to do.
— No thanks. I like to get my bad breath from pepperoni pizza.
— Thanks, but if I'm going to ruin my body, I'll do it with a hot fudge sundae.
— No, but do you happen to have any milk? I'm on a program to build brain cells.

What Would You Do?
Decision-Making and Discussion

This activity teaches children to:

— differentiate right choices from wrong choices.
— identify different methods of evaluating behavior.
— recognize inner conflict over doing the right thing.
— describe times when they did the right thing.

You will need:

several 3X5 cards for each child; chart paper

Directions:

Begin by explaining to your child/children that this activity is about how decisions are made, and about deciding to do what's right in situations that call for moral judgment. In your own words state:

Every time you take an action of any kind, that action is preceded by a decision. So you are making decisions constantly. Sometimes the decisions seem automatic, like the decision to sit at the dinner table, or wave to a friend across the street. Other times, the decision requires some thought. Maybe you have different choices, like whether to study or play games on your computer. However, if you were told not to play games until your homework was finished, then it would be right to study, and wrong to play games. Many decisions involve choosing between right and wrong behaviors. Sometimes the difference between right and wrong is very clear. Other times it is more difficult to figure out.

Present the following dilemma:

You are in a store with two friends, Chris and Lee, looking at some neat merchandise. Lee disappears down a nearby aisle. After a few minutes, you decide to join Lee. When you turn the corner, you see Lee slip a package into his backpack. You also see a store employee a few yards away who apparently saw the same thing you did. You stop in your tracks and quickly back up, wondering what to do.

Ask, *What are your choices?*

List all ideas on the chart paper. Encourage numerous possibilities, including:
- Go back and rejoin Chris, hoping the store employee didn't notice you.
- Go back, grab Chris and head for the door, hoping that Lee will be all right and will join you later.
- Grab Lee and run for the door.
- Walk over and quietly urge Lee to put the package back because someone is watching.
- Urge Lee to put the package back because stealing is wrong.
- Try to distract the employee with a question.
- Stand your ground and wait to see what happens. If the employee confronts Lee, tell the truth about what you saw.
- Wait to see what happens. If the employee intervenes, pretend you don't know Lee.

When your child/children run out of ideas, go back and discuss the options. Talk about what's right and wrong with each idea, and what might happen as a result of each choice. Determine with your child/children the best and right decision to be made and write it on the chart paper. If home schooling one child, follow the directions above with Story 1 and Story 2.

If home schooling a group of children, distribute the 3x5 cards. Read aloud Story 1 below. Give the children a few minutes to write down on a card a brief description of what they would do. Collect the cards and read each one aloud and discuss what might happen because of that choice. After all the choices have been read and discussed, write the decisions that are appropriate and morally correct on the chart paper.

Again, engage the children in a discussion about what's right and wrong in the situation, and the possible consequences of various choices.

Follow the same procedure with Story 2.

Story 1

When Mr. and Mrs. Greer go on vacation for three weeks, they ask Kim to feed their cat, Sydney, twice a day. They also ask her to water their houseplants. They offer to pay Kim $10 a week and she agrees. Every morning before school, Kim stops by the Greer house. Sydney is always waiting for his breakfast near the back door. In the evening, she returns, feeds the cat his dinner, and checks to see if anything needs watering. For the first two weeks, Kim sticks to this routine. However, during the third week, Kim herself has vacation from school and sleeps later than usual. On Monday and Tuesday, she doesn't get around to feeding Sydney his breakfast until 10:00 a.m. and forgets to check the plants. On Wednesday, she stops briefly at noon before rushing off to a friend's house. On Thursday, Kim goes to a movie in the evening and forgets to feed the cat his dinner. When she goes over on Friday morning, Sydney isn't at the back door and doesn't answer her call. Friday evening, Sydney is in the yard, but doesn't seem hungry.

When the Greers arrive home on Sunday, they pay Kim and ask how everything went. She tells them, "Fine." On Monday evening, the Greers phone and ask Kim to come next door and answer some questions. They ask Kim why Sydney showed up hungry at another neighbor's house several times during the previous week, and why two of their favorite house plants are dry and wilted. Kim acts surprised and tells them she has no idea why. She insists that she did everything they asked her to do. If you were Kim, what would you do?

Story 2

Mark gets his parents' permission to walk home from town through a scenic canyon with his friend Henry, rather than take the regular route on the sidewalk. Though Mark promises to stay on the hiking trails, Henry talks him into taking a short cut up a rugged canyon wall to their neighborhood. Part way up, the boys are attacked by a swarm of bees. The bees chase and sting them. Henry, who doesn't run as fast as Mark, gets the worst of it. At the first house they come to, they are given shelter and first aid, and the owner calls their parents, police and medics. While the medics are preparing to take Henry to the hospital, Henry whispers tearfully to Mark not to tell anyone they went off the trail. The police officer wants to know where the attack took place so he can send an exterminator to kill the bees and determine if the hive belonged to dangerous Africanized or killer bees. Mark's parents want reassurance that their son obeyed their orders. Mark is torn. He doesn't think it's fair to kill the bees. If he says he and Henry were on the trail, the exterminator probably won't find the hive and he and Henry won't get into any trouble. But if they don't find the hive, they won't know if the bees are Africanized. He's also worried about Henry, whose father is very strict. If you were Mark, what would you do?

Conclude the activity with a culminating discussion.

Questions for Discussion and Reflection:

1. Why is it sometimes hard to make the right decision?
2. How often has fear of punishment, or fear of the consequences, caused you to make a wrong decision?
3. What determines whether a decision is right or wrong?
4. When should you ask for help in making a decision?
5. Does it take more courage to do the wrong thing and worry about getting caught, or to do the right thing and accept the consequences?

A Time I "Took My Medicine"

A Sharing Circle

This Sharing Circle teaches children to:

— explain the connection between an action and its consequences.
— describe how they benefit by taking responsibility for their mistakes.

Introduce the Topic:

Have you ever heard the expression, "take your medicine?" It means that when you do something wrong or make a mistake, you have to be ready to take the consequences. Today we're going to talk about times when we accepted our medicine because we knew we deserved it. The topic is, "A Time I 'Took My Medicine.'"

Think of a time when you did something wrong or against the rules, or simply made a bad mistake. It doesn't matter whether you did it on purpose or accidentally. In either case, you accepted the consequences without whining, or making excuses, or blaming someone else. Maybe you were punished for going somewhere that you were told not to go, or perhaps you had too many fouls in basketball and had to leave the game. Maybe you didn't do your homework or finish a report, and accepted the consequences without grumbling about it. Or perhaps you were punished for lying or fighting. Think about it for a few moments, and then tell us what happened and how you reacted. The topic is, "A Time I 'Took My Medicine.'"

Questions for Discussion and Reflection:

1. Why is it better to accept the consequences of your actions instead of trying to get away with something wrong?
2. What would it be like if everyone tried to get away with breaking the rules and doing bad things?
3. Does it take courage to admit your mistakes and take the consequences? Explain.
4. Is deciding to "take your medicine" often a choice you can make in response to a mistake you've made?
5. How can admitting your mistakes and "taking your medicine" make you a better person?

A Time I Kept My Promise
A Sharing Circle

This Sharing Circle teaches children to:

—explain the value of keeping promises.
—associate feelings with honesty.
—associate honesty with the development of trust.

Introduce the Topic:

Today's topic is, "A Time I Kept My Promise." Have you ever made a promise to someone and kept it? You said that you were going to do something, or not do something, and you decided to follow through — even though it might have taken some hard work. Maybe you promised your dad that you would sweep the kitchen or patio, and you did it. Perhaps you made a promise to a friend that you would go to his house on a Saturday to help with math homework and you went, even though you had to give up a more enjoyable activity. Or perhaps you promised not to do something, like not to fight with your sister or brother when the two of you were alone. How did you feel about keeping your word? Did anyone notice or acknowledge you for keeping your promise? Try to remember a time that you made a promise and kept it, and get ready to share it with the group. The topic is, "A Time I Kept My Promise."

Questions for Discussion and Reflection:

1. Why is it important to keep promises when we make them?
2. How does it feel when someone makes a promise to you and keeps it? ...doesn't keep it?
3. How does keeping, or not keeping, promises affect the willingness of others to trust you?

What Did You Learn About Making Good Decisions?

Use this page to think about and record the things you have learned about making good decisions. You can write, draw pictures, scribble and doodle, create a poem, or anything else that has meaning to you and will help you remember what you have learned.

When you finish, show this page to someone else and explain what you have learned.

If your heart is in Social-Emotional Learning, visit us online.

Come see us at
www.InnerchoicePublishing.com

Our web site gives you a look at all our other Social-Emotional Learning-based books, free activities, articles, research, and learning and teaching strategies. Every week you'll get a new Sharing Circle topic and lesson.

15079 Oak Chase Court
Wellington, FL 33414